Hand in Hand with Hanon

by
Buddy DeFranco

1st Edition
1996

Copyright © 1996 by Buddy DeFranco
P. O. Box 252
Sunnyside Beach, FL 32461

All rights reserved. No part of this book may be reproduced or transmitted in any form or by any means,
electric or mechanical, including photocopying, recording, or by any information storage
and retrieval system, without permission in writing from the Publisher.

Printed in the United States of America By
Sparks Printing & Graphics
Tupelo, Mississippi

ISBN: 0-9654244-0-5
Library of Congress Catalog Card Number: 96-97165

Forward

Hand in Hand with Hanon
Buddy De Franco

    For many years I've been intrigued by the Hanon exercises for piano.

    Almost all of the really professional pianists I've met studied the Hanon Exercises.

    It has been an idea of mine to transcribe these exercises for the clarinet; moreover, write them in all twelve keys. I did this first for my own practice sessions then, in time realized that this would make an excellent group of studies to compliment any other studies for most instruments.

    So, here it is - I put together my original book, "On Jazz Improvisation", with these Hanon studies which I feel really go "Hand in Hand."

Buddy De Franco

*Special thanks to
Keith Perkins, Wick Sparks & Joyce DeFranco
for making this book possible.*

Preface

In the early days of jazz, the music used as a basis for improvising consisted principally of the Blues with its simplest harmonies, compositions related in form and harmonic characteristics to marches and to Ragtime, and popular tunes based primarily on "barber shop" harmonies. The ad-lib artist could get by with no formal knowledge in the field of harmony. The only requirements were a fairly good ear, a moderate amount of technique, and a familiarity with a comparatively few harmonic progressions–and a great amount of imaginaton and inventiveness.

Today the situation is quite different. To be successful, the musician in the jazz field needs extensive schooling in theory, harmony, form, etc. He needs to be well informed in contemporary concepts in the building of complex chords, in the application of modal scales, and in the utilization of meters other than the standard four-in-a-measure employed for so many years. In addition, he needs the creative ability to combine his musical knowledge and experience with something of himself in order to express himself with a degree of originality.

In this book, my aim is to provide important information slanted toward modern jazz as played on the clarinet. Much of the material given is not to be found in any other clarinet books.

In addition to instruction related directly to the playing of modern jazz, I have included a good deal of essential information concerned with basic clarinet playing, and applicable to the performance of any style of music. We refer here to the factors involved in good tone production and the development of a mature technique.

The ambitious student will take a giant step toward the achievement of his goal as a competent exponent of modern jazz by taking seriously all of the study material presented here.

Buddy De Franco

Table of Contents

	Page
Forward	iii
Preface	iv

Section A:

Clarinet practice; tonal characteristics and registers of the clarinets	1
Modern jazz and the clarinet	2
Analysis and comparison	3
Standards for modern jazz; Free form jazz	5

Section B:

Scales and intervals	7
Scale studies	12

Section C:

Chords	21
Inversions; altered chords	22
Resolutions of chords; tests	24
Extended Chords	27
Chord symbol equivalents	29
Rhythm	31
Scale studies	33

Section D:

Hanon Exercises	41
Exercise 1	43
Exercise 2	47
Exercise 3	51
Exercise 4	53
Exercise 5	59
Exercise 6	63
Exercise 7	67
Exercise 8	71
Exercise 9	75
Exercise 10	79
Exercise 11	83
Exercise 12	87
Exercise 13	91
Exercise 14	96
Exercise 15	101
Exercise 16	106
Exercise 17	111
Exercise 18	116
Exercise 19	121
Exercise 20	133
Chromatic Exercises	145

Section E:
- Modern jazz improvising; vibrato; form; test 153
- Blues in F 156
- Blues in C 157
- * Blues progression with melodic line 159
- Blues in C concert 162
- Recommendations on interpretation and construction of the "line"; larger jazz forms 164
- First endings; second endings 165
- Test in G 167
- Technical study; Melody in G 169
- Test in D 171
- Superimposed chords; Melody in D 173
- * A Blues construction in C concert 174
- The clarinet as related to concert key 176
- Dual chord symbols 178
- Jazz in three-four meter 180
- Jazz in five-four meter 181
- Concluding remarks 182
- * Max is Back 183
- * Lake Five 190
- * Chloe's Odyssey 194
- * Flathead Blues 204

*DeFranco originals scored for small groups

Section A

Clarinet Practice

Many students ask, "How long each day should I practice?" The answer is–as much as you can. However, I feel that practicing beyond the point of general fatigue is a waste of time and energy. If you have already practiced possibly two hours and feel physically and mentally tired, any further practice would be merely a ritualistic or automatic playing of the lesson without full concentration. I consider this a waste.

I suggest practicing half-hour to one-hour periods several times each day.

As you develop, keep in mind that consistent jazz playing without also assiduous study each day of the fundamentals and "classical" technique *will eventually destroy your playing*. Despite the fact that jazz music affords many benefits, such as freedom, imagination, pulse, intensity, etc., without strict adherence to basics, one can lose tone, technique, and a necessary degree of self discipline, which I deem important for all music.

Furthermore, it is necessary not only to become completely familiar with the clarinet, but also to become "musical." To reach this goal, I recommend that in addition to the amount of time you spend becoming technically proficient with the clarinet, you spend an equal amount of time with ear training to develop a sound harmonic sense. This is an important prerequisite for playing the clarinet (or any other musical instrument).

This means, for those of us who are interested in playing jazz especially with a single note instrument, that we must constantly make ourselves aware of harmonies, scales, syncopation, and last but not least, swing or jazz rhythms and/or pulse. The jazz or swing concept cannot actually be taught. It must be absorbed by the student through the process of constantly listening to good jazz artists and playing with other competent jazz players as much as possible.

Tonal Characteristics and Registers of the Clarinet

The sound of the clarinet is produced by the vibration of the reed. The instrument proper acts as a tube, the effective length of which may be altered at the will of the player (by means of his fingers) to produce sounds of different pitches. Much of the sound of the instrument is transmitted through the tone holes–the holes under the fingers or those that can be opened or closed by means of keys. Low E is sounded entirely through the bell. Middle B sounds either completely or substantially through the bell. Because the tiny hole used for the register key is open when middle B is played, it is likely that a small portion of the sound comes through this hole.

The unique sound of the clarinet results from the fact that its bore, except for the portion in and near the bell, is substantially cylindrical. The saxophone, oboe and bassoon have a conical bore. In the case of the conical instruments, all of the members of the harmonic series (overtones) are relatively strong. With the clarinet, however, the octave and some of the other overtones (in a definite pattern) are quite weak. Because of this, the clarinet has a tone quality in a class all its own, and is said to be built in "twelfths" rather than in octaves as are the conical instruments.

While on the conical instruments the thumb key is called an octave key, on the clarinet it must properly be called a "register" key, since the sound produced by using this key is not an octave higher than the related lower sound, but rather is a twelfth higher. For instance, if you play low F on the clarinet, pressing the register key gives you middle C. This is twelve (natural) notes higher than the low F first played.

It must be explained here that "jazz playing" as such also requires a percussive attack and "feel", therefore the setup of mouthpiece and reed must differ greatly from the typical "legit" facing and reed.

For best practical "jazz" results, I use an open facing Bari BDF No. 3 with 4½ strength John Denman reeds.

I would never recommend such a setup for legitimate playing. Moreover, it would be impossible.

The compass of the clarinet contains four portions, called registers. Each has a tone color somewhat of its own.

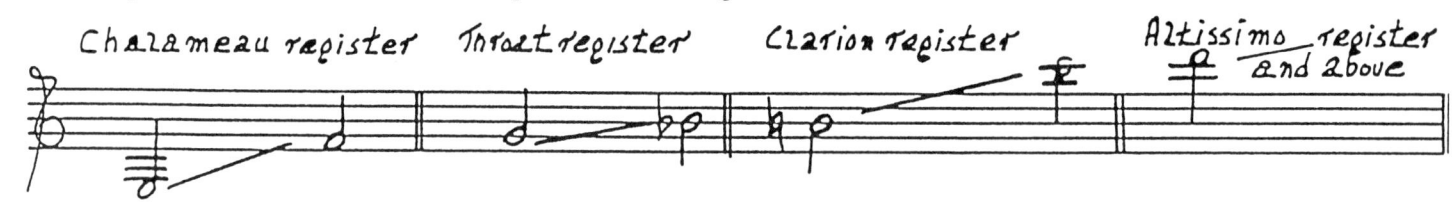

[Musical notation showing four registers: Chalameau register, Throat register, Clarion register, Altissimo register and above]

Because of the unusual tonal characteristics of the clarinet, it is more difficult to record than most other instruments. If there are flaws in a recording, or if the motor speed in a record player is not precisely uniform, the clarinet sound is noticeably affected. The sound is bubbly, and gives the impression that it was recorded under water.

Modern Jazz and the Clarinet

I would like first to make some issues clear regarding the "Modern Jazz" form. Despite the variety of modern jazz forms being exploited today, for instance, "cool", "hard swing", "soul", "outside," etc., it is my opinion that all music must have three basic ingredients:
1. Good tone production;
2. Good facility; i.e., technique.
3. Expression and/or concept.

Now we will analyze these three. First, tone production. There are essentially two types of tone quality.
   a. A strong, full and vibrant quality.
   b. A light, delicate kind of airy or ethereal quality.

Regardless of which tone quality you prefer, the basic requirements are the same–even quality and accuracy, good intonation, and positive or consistent temper in tone production. This can be obtained only by long tone practice, however boring it may be, and consistent study of slow legato and melodic passages.

Regarding facility or technique, again two schools of thought come to mind–the soft, quiet and "liquid" technique as contrasted with a strong pulsative or percussive technique. Regardless of which you prefer, it is absolutely necessary for you to pursue assiduously the study of scales, arpeggios and intervals.

The third ingredient, expression and concept, is the most elusive one. First off, one can say that Heifetz has expression, or "Bird" was expressive, or contemporary Indian music is expressive. What I am driving at here is that everyone can use the argument that expression in any given musical form depends on the receptivity and perception of the listener; therefore, who is to say what is expressive, or even good or bad? I believe that this reasoning or justification of what one prefers can ultimately lead to chaos.

In the area of interpretation, and ultimately expression, I believe we must, as in all art forms, establish a standard from which to work and develop. Let us pursue this further. Jazz, and specifically "modern jazz," like any art form, consists of transmitting thought and expression by means of a tangible or perceptible medium so that other people can derive an emotional experience.

Now this emotional experience in modern jazz breaks down into two basic factors, and these are perceived by two basic functions of the human being.

One is mental or intellectual experience. The other is physical or somatic experience.

From my personal observation, one form of jazz, the "cool" music and "third stream" music appeals basically to the intellect. That is to say, the emotional experience is derived predominately from the intellect.

The "soul" or "hard swing" has its basic roots in the physical or somatic experience where the dominant role is played by the rhythmic pulse and the intellectual aspect is secondary.

"Rock and Roll" as an example of music is completely physical or somatic with little regard for the intellect. We could go into a lengthly discussion regarding Rock and Roll satisfying a particular "emotional need" of the teenager. However, our aim is to deal only with modern jazz, the art form per se.

Back to modern jazz. Many people believe now that modern jazz and symphonic or classical music will eventually integrate and be one and the same. This noble thought has its ramifications.

First off, although modern jazz requires facility, it must of necessity break classical rules in order to give it tangible expression. Secondly, jazz cannot be hamstrung with classical orchestration. So by the time you allow enough freedom for jazz in the orchestration and further allow the jazz soloist to break the "rules" of the classical form, you no longer have classical or jazz, but rather a combination of incompatible entities, like oil and water.

Now let me qualify the above statement. It is definitely possible to combine successfully within the framework of any given composition both the classical and jazz forms, passing from one to the other in a specific sequence, but one or the other must crystallize separately. To this day, there are relatively <u>few</u> genuine "crossover" artists.

So I feel relatively safe in saying that jazz will be refined many times over, but will remain a jazz art form. Likewise, classical music will remain a separate entity in the world of the arts.

Let me add that in the above discussion I am using the term "classical music" as a generalization, more or less in the language of the layman, to include all symphonic and concert music of all periods–Baroque, Classical, Romantic, French Modern, Modern and Contemporary periods (atonal and polytonal music, twelve-tone, quarter tone, etc.)

Analysis and Comparison

Jazz is improvising on a theme [eg: theme and variation] utilizing all, or in part
    African-American rhythms
    Latin-American
    European harmonies and scales, plus chords
    2nd scales developed by the American Jazz players
    Eastern scales - harmonies - Eastern rhythms

to "create" your own "improvised" musical story.

Before we can arrive at a satisfactory basis for the extemporaneous playing of jazz in the modern form, we need to explore briefly the earlier forms of jazz.

In the case of Dixieland and Swing forms, relatively few harmonic devices were employed, and the ad-lib player was concerned predominately with vertical allusions to the chord structure. For example, if the chord pattern given below was employed as the framework,

The ad-lib player might run through a group of arpeggios with relatively few alterations–

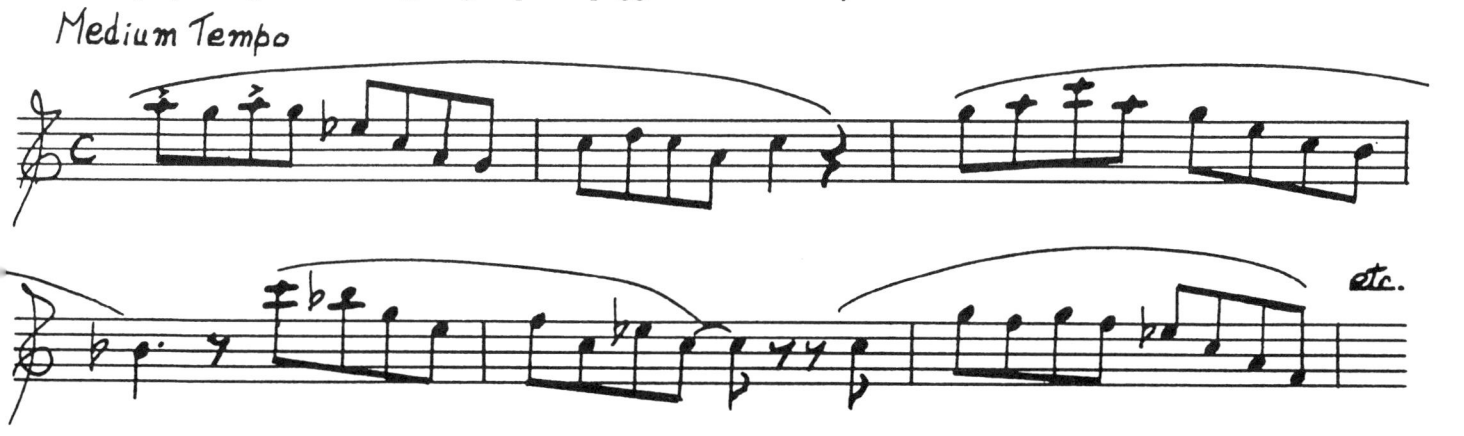

Here the emphasis is vertical with relatively few alterations.

Now although we must have arpeggios based on chord structures at our command, we must think in terms of more alterations and in terms of "linear" expression, or the "horizontal line."

Let's increase the number of alterations and use extensions of the chords, and try to develop the "line" utilizing the same basic chord structure.

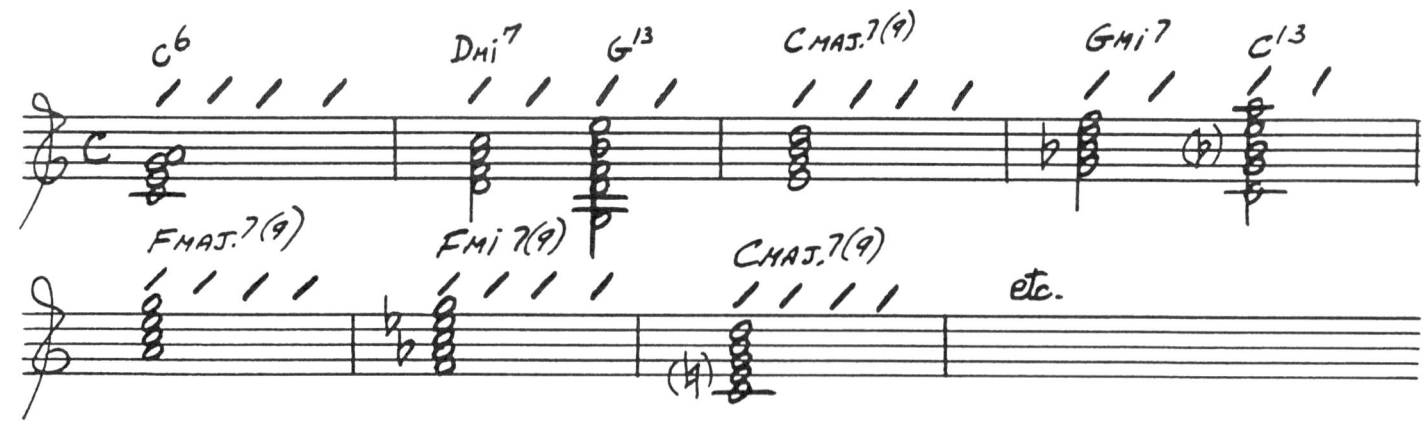

We might develop a line with these new alterations.

Now our line looks like this. The emphasis is horizontal; i.e., "linear."

If the reader is unable to comprehend fully the chords employed here, I recommend a careful and complete study of the explanations given later in this book.

Standards for Modern Jazz

Let me now emphasize my statement that standards must of necessity be realized or developed as a prerequisite for playing modern jazz. Some comparisons are in order.

In preparing for the opera, the singer must study long and hard to develop the voice to be rich, full and accurate to meet prescribed standards of refinement. He or she must also develop a technique so that he is able to sing complex passages with ease. Finally, he must learn to transform inner expression to real and tangible expression to establish contact with his audiences.

Similarly, in the classical field the musician must develop his tone to a rich and vibrant quality. He or she must practice many hours to develop his technical facility. And finally, he must be able to express emotion through his instrument to establish contact with the listener and fuse with the orchestra.

Since both the aforementioned art forms are much older than jazz, they have become refined and innovators over the centuries have provided new and higher standards for others to utilize as guideposts.

I believe that jazz is going through the same "growing pains" and precisely the same developmental stages. It is becoming more complex and exacting. It is making greater demends on the player. It is definitely becoming more and more expressive.

The age when a jazz artist could blindly stumble along with the aid of his ear alone and a bottle of whiskey in order to "say something" with his instrument is fast disappearing. Since more stringent demends both technically and harmonically are being imposed on the ad-lib artist, he must refine and develop to its maximum his musical potential. It is my aim, therefore, to help the musician become better equipped and better prepared to employ his talent and instrument for the ultimate expression of our modern jazz art form, and that it has become, in terms of music theory, the balance of psyche and soma; that is, both physical and intellectual in its expression.

Let me emphasize that it is not my aim to teach the ad-lib performer how to "swing." This cannot be done. My aims is to provide the tools with which to perform our tasks better.

Since development of the ear is a prerequisite for playing all music generally and is absolutely essential for the modern jazz ad-lib player, it is necessary for the musician to learn all the scales, major and minor, by ear in every key. He must also learn and recognize all chord alterations and superimpositions. He must also thorughly learn intervals by "ear." He must learn to recognize and spell the tonality of any given passage of music and to understand the relationship of what he is playing to the total chord picture. Finally, he must learn "time sequences" and rhythmic patterns and develop the pulse in his playing. All the subtleties and nuances must be left to the player's individual talents and creativity.

A really thorough background in the essentials of basic music is an absolute must. A convenient way to achieve this is a thorough study of a book I consider to be the finest in its field: "Elementary Training For Musicians" by Paul Hindemith. Don't let the word elementary in the title fool you. When you get into the book you will see what I mean.

To young, aspiring musicians I recommend as follows–don't put the cart before the horse. Let's not give way to the desire and temptation to play jazz without the basic foundation to carry it off properly. Let us first have at our command all the knowledge and facility necessary to support the creative faculty. Then we can utilize our ingenuity to the fullest, and, like a fine orator or writer, "say" what we want to say.

If we all work toward this end, we will see the refinements that will set up for us our standards in modern jazz.

Free Form Jazz

I believe that some exponents of the present Free Form or "Outside" Jazz are somewhat lacking in knowledge of theory and harmony in comparison with the writers in the symphonic and concert fields who are substantially going after the same results. I refer to those such as Alban Berg, Arnold Schoenberg and other Twelve-Tone and Tone-Row exponents. However, the Free Form Jazz group does represent a force, and I believe they will provide another avenue of approach to jazz. But only those jazz exponents who are basically equipped with the sound fundamentals will succeed. Free Form Jazz is not enough without basic studies and self-disciplinary measures that give all great music validity and direction.

The element of chance is not enough to give validity to music. I will quote Oscar Peterson, who says, "Experiments should be conducted at rehearsals and have no place in the performance."

Section B
Scales and Intervals

Since improvising is based largely on scales, intervals and chords, a thorough knowledge of these subjects is necessary.

A scale is a succession of tones progressing upwards or downwards that makes up the basic musical material on which a composition or improvisation is based. There are many types of scales that have been used throughout the history of civilization and in various parts of the world. We need to concern ourselves with only a few of these.

Each scale of no matter what type has a principal note from which it is named. This is very often the melody note on which the piece of music comes to a close, and is called the "keynote" or "tonic." We will deal first with the most familiar type of scale, the "major" scale. This consists of five whole-steps and two half-steps arranged in a definite order. In the C major scale shown, the order of the whole and half-steps is indicated. Notice that each individual scale member is assigned a Roman numeral.

Whole Step	Whole Step	Half Step	Whole Step	Whole Step	Whole Step	Half Step
C	D	E	F	G	A	B	C
I	II	III	IV	V	VI	VII	VIII (I)

Degrees

The individual scale members, called "degrees of the scale," have names as well as numbers.

As already mentioned, the first degree (1) is called the tonic. - [Ionian scale]*

The second degree (II) is the supertonic. - [Dorian scale]*

The third degree (III) is the mediant. - [Phyrigian scale]*

The fourth degree (IV) is the subdominant. - [Lydian scale]*

The fifth degree (V) is the dominant. - [Mixalidian scale]*

The sixth degree (VI) is the submediant. - [Aolian scale]*

The seventh degree (VII) is the leading tone. - [Locrian scale]*

> *These are the names of the Modal scales based on each degree of the major scale.

The eighth degree (VIII) is called the octave, and is a note with the same letter name as the tonic. For practical purposes, we will not call this note the octave; rather, we will consider it to be the tonic sounded higher.

Play the C major scale and notice the difference in sound between the whole-steps and the half-steps. Next, play the following skips:

C to D (I to II; tonic to supertonic).

C to E (I to III; tonic to mediant).

C to F (I to IV; Tonic to subdominant).

C to G (I to V; tonic to dominant).

C to A (I to VI; tonic to submediant).

C to B (I to VII; tonic to leading tone).

C to C (I to VIII or to I sounded higher; tonic to octave).

Notice that these skips are progressively larger. The size of the skip (difference in pitch) between two notes played either successively or simultaneously is called the "interval" between the notes.

It is extremely important for you to have a clear picture of what an interval is, since the whole subject of chord construction is based on the intervals between the component notes of chords.

A logical approach to the study of intervals is the careful consideration of the size of the skips between the tonic and the various other members of the C major scale, such as you have just played. To clarify this point, we give you again each skip that you played and show the expression signifying the size of the skip, or intervals between the two notes played.

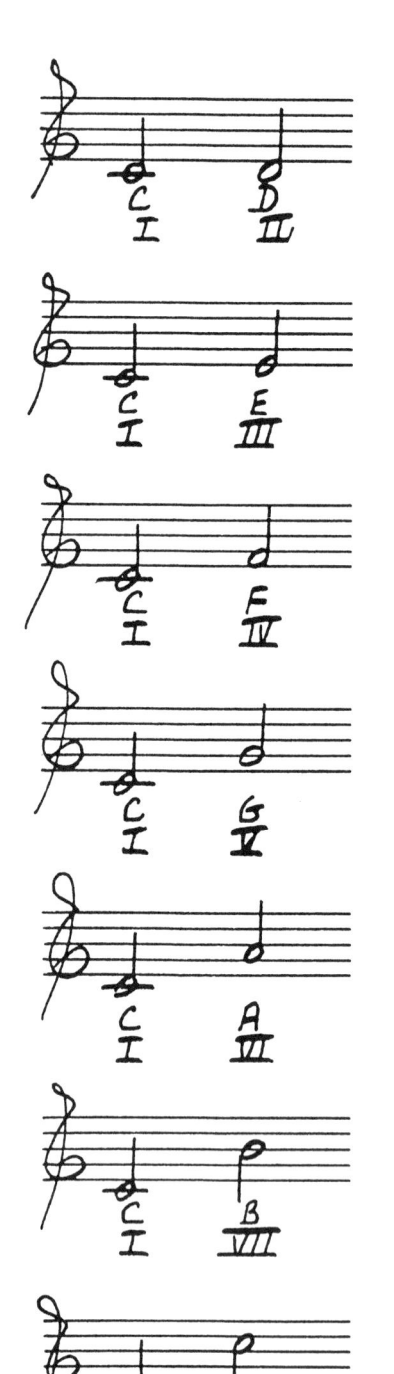

The interval between C and D (I and II) is a "major second." It contains one whole-step, which equals two half-steps.

The interval between C and E (I and III) is a "major third," containing two whole-steps (four half-steps).

C to F (I to IV) is a "perfect fourth": two whole-steps plus one-half step, or five half-steps.

C to G (I to V) is a "perfect fifth"; three whole-steps plus one half-step, or seven half-steps.

C to A (I to VI) is a "major sixth"; four whole-steps plus one-half step, or nine half-steps.

C to B (I to VII) is a "major seventh"; five whole-steps plus one half-step, or eleven half-steps.

C to C (I to VIII) is a "perfect octave"; five whole-steps plus two half-steps, or twelve half-steps.

Finally, play this passage slowly, and try to remember the name and sound of each interval. Also, try singing the intervals.

[Musical staff showing: Major Second, Major Third, Perfect fourth, Perfect fifth]

[Musical staff showing: Major Sixth, Major Seventh, Octave]

For the most part, we will figure the size of intervals from the lower note upwards. Obviously, the interval between any pair of notes is the same size whether figured from the lower to the upper, or from the upper downwards to the lower. Be sure to bear in mind that any interval may be constructed either upwards or downwards from any note. You will be able to figure intervals readily only after a considerable amount of study and experience.

By the use of flats and sharps, we may construct intervals of sizes other than those so far shown. In order to understand them, you need to study very carefully all of the following information. We will show how you can alter the size of an interval by altering the second note in each pair.

A major interval, when reduced in size by a half-step, becomes minor (lower the second note).

A perfect interval, when enlarged by a half-step, becomes augmented (raise the second note).

A perfect interval, when reduced by a half-step, becomes diminished (lower the second note).

(A minor interval, when enlarged by a half-step, becomes major.)

Next we have, in chart form, all the intervals you have previously studied together with many intervals formed by altering the second note in the pair. It will require quite a bit of study to master all of this information. Some intervals are exactly the same size as others, but are written differently. You will see this when you compare the sizes of the intervals expressed in terms of the number of half-steps contained, as shown in parenthesis.

[Musical staff showing: Minor 2nd (1), Major 2nd (2), Augmented 2nd (3), Minor 3rd (3)]

[Musical staff showing: Major 3rd (4), Perfect 4th (5), Augmented 4th (6), Diminished 5th (6)]

[Musical staff showing: Perfect 5th (7), Augmented 5th (8), Minor 6th (8), Major 6th (9)]

[Musical staff showing: Augmented 6th (10), Minor 7th (10), Major 7th (11), Octave (12)]

For the sake of expediency, some musicians call the augmented 11th the "flatted fifth".

To carry this matter further, we now need to show a chart of intervals larger than an octave. These large intervals are of prime importance to us, since through their use we build chord extensions, which are the backbone of modern jazz harmony.

Minor 9th (13)   Major 9th (14)   Augmented 9th (15)   Minor 10th (15)

Major 10th (16)   Perfect 11th (17)   Augmented 11th (18)   Perfect 12th (19)   Major 13th (20)

Play the music in the two interval charts slowly. Remember the names of the intervals and their sound. Sing the intervals if you can. Train your ear to hear them. (An old saying: "If we can't hear it, we can't really play it.")

I advise all students to play these intervals on the piano and to become relatively familiar with the keyboard. Try eventually to learn all intervals in all keys.

In addition to a knowledge of intervals, we must become thoroughly versed in all scales—major, minor and chromatic.

Each major scale has its relative minor scale. The keynote of the relative minor is the interval of a minor third below the tonic of the major scale, which makes it the submediant of the major scale.

In common use today are two types of minor scales, the melodic and the harmonic. In the case of the melodic minor, the pattern in descending is not the same as in ascending. The harmonic minor uses the same pattern in both directions. Study the music below.

C Major Scale

Melodic A Minor Scale   (relative to C Major)

Harmonic A Minor Scale   (also relative to C Major)

Chromatic Scale

There are also "model" scales, based on the ancient Greek modes. Here are two examples.

Dorian Mode

Lydian Mode

In addition, we have the following.

The Pentatonic Scale

The Whole-tone Scale

Many of the modern jazz figures used today are based on the Dorian mode. Although we read D6 or D13 and, of course, the basic tonality is D major, we see in melodic lines and in ad-lib variations a D minor mode as well.

Example   with   Dorian modal scale

We will, later on, use this sequence to try some jazz patterns extemporaneously.

Example

Slowly

Medium

Medium

The above are all against a D *major tonality*!

Although some modern jazz is based on the modal scales, the subject is too complex to explore further at this point. Also, we shall see that our individual scale patterns are predominantly based on our harmonic devices and therefore we will be more concerned with harmony as a point of reference.

The scale studies on the next pages are to be played first by note (reading) and finally from memory, or "by ear." Daily practice of this material is essential. When you have these scales completely under control, you may then devise or invent your own scale patterns to develop further your ear and technique.

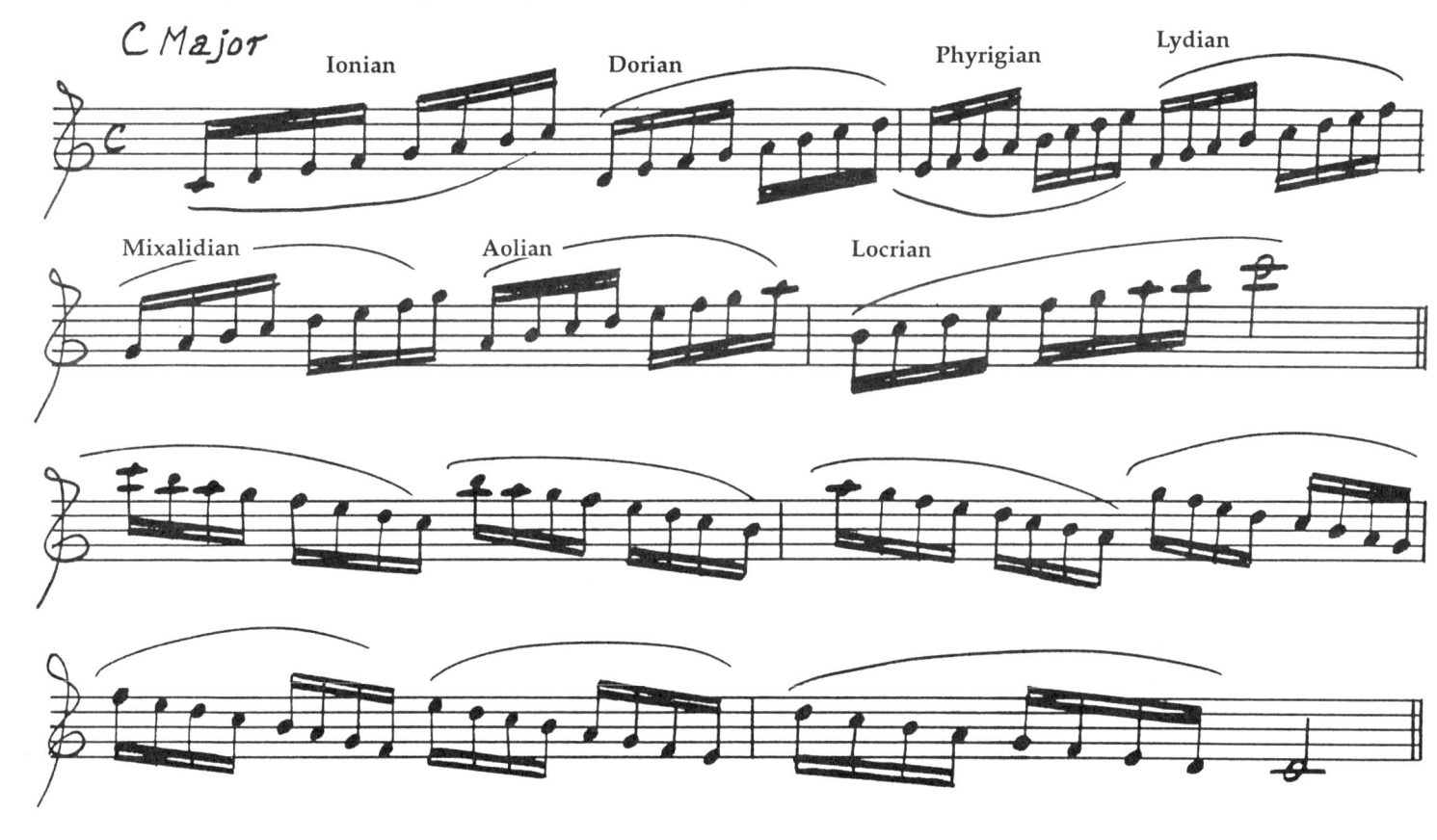

The articulation may be changed and varied to help develop a better technique. Here are a few examples.

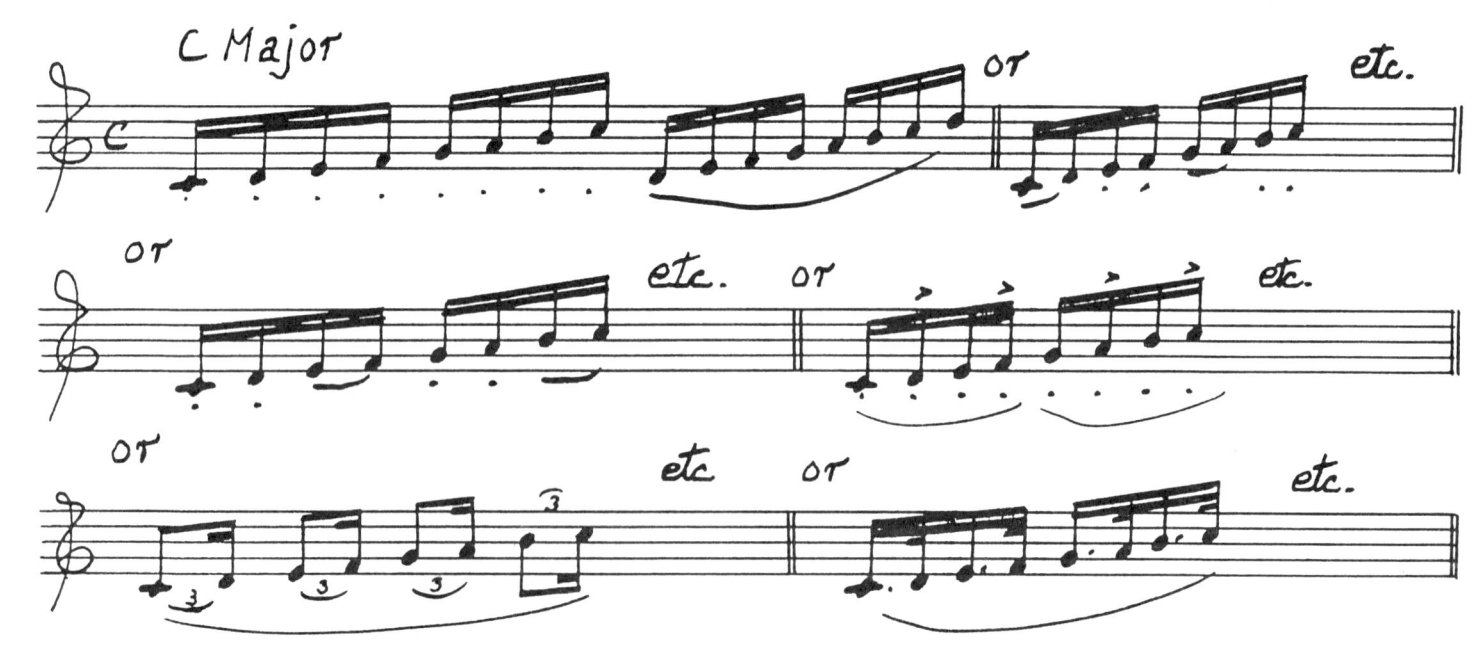

The explanation of melodic minor scale construction has already been given.

F Major

D Minor

B♭ Major

G Minor

Eb Major

C Minor

G Major

E Minor

D Major

B Minor

A Major

F# Minor

E Major

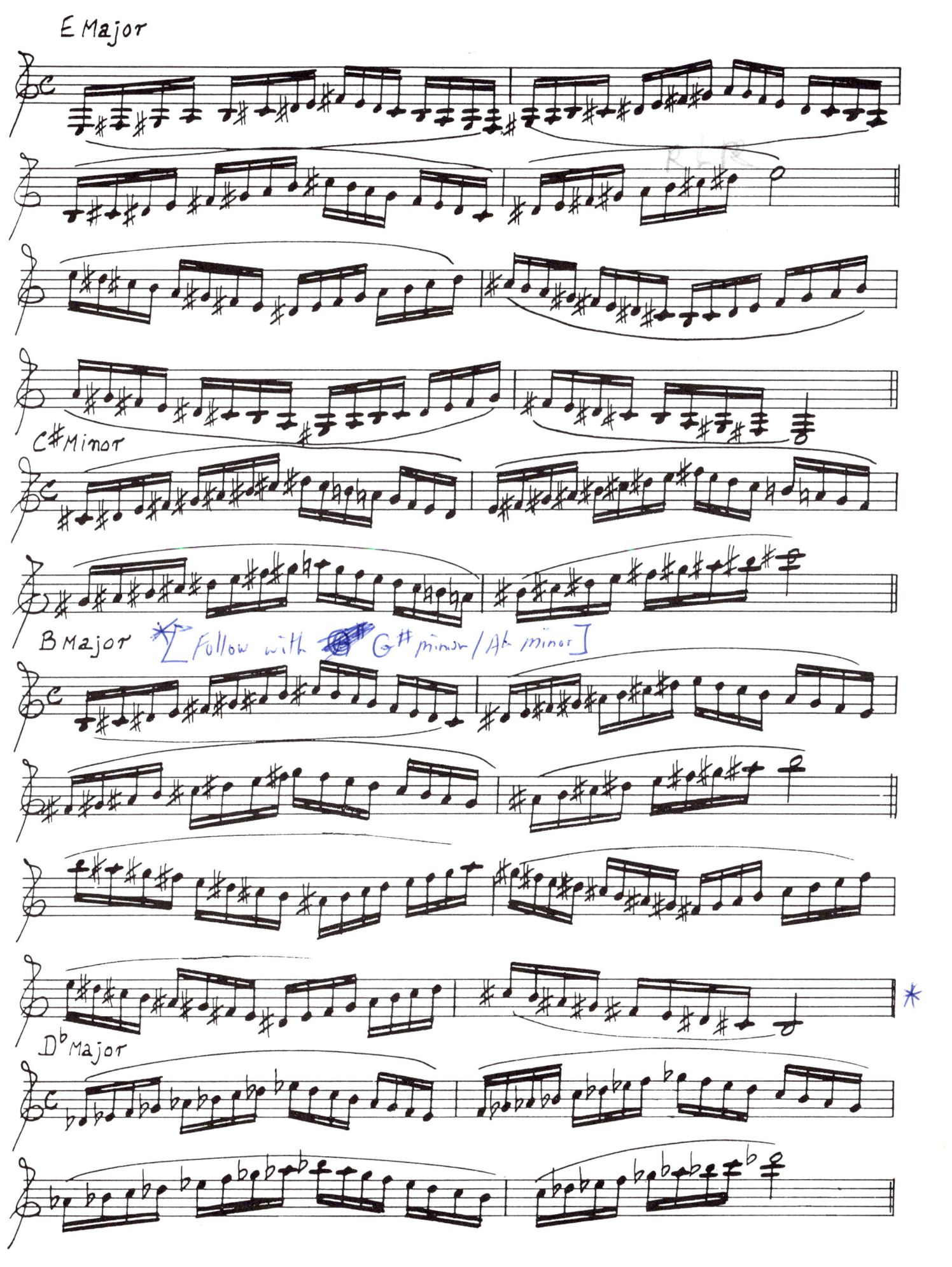

C# Minor

B Major [Follow with G# minor/Ab minor]

Db Major

B♭ Minor

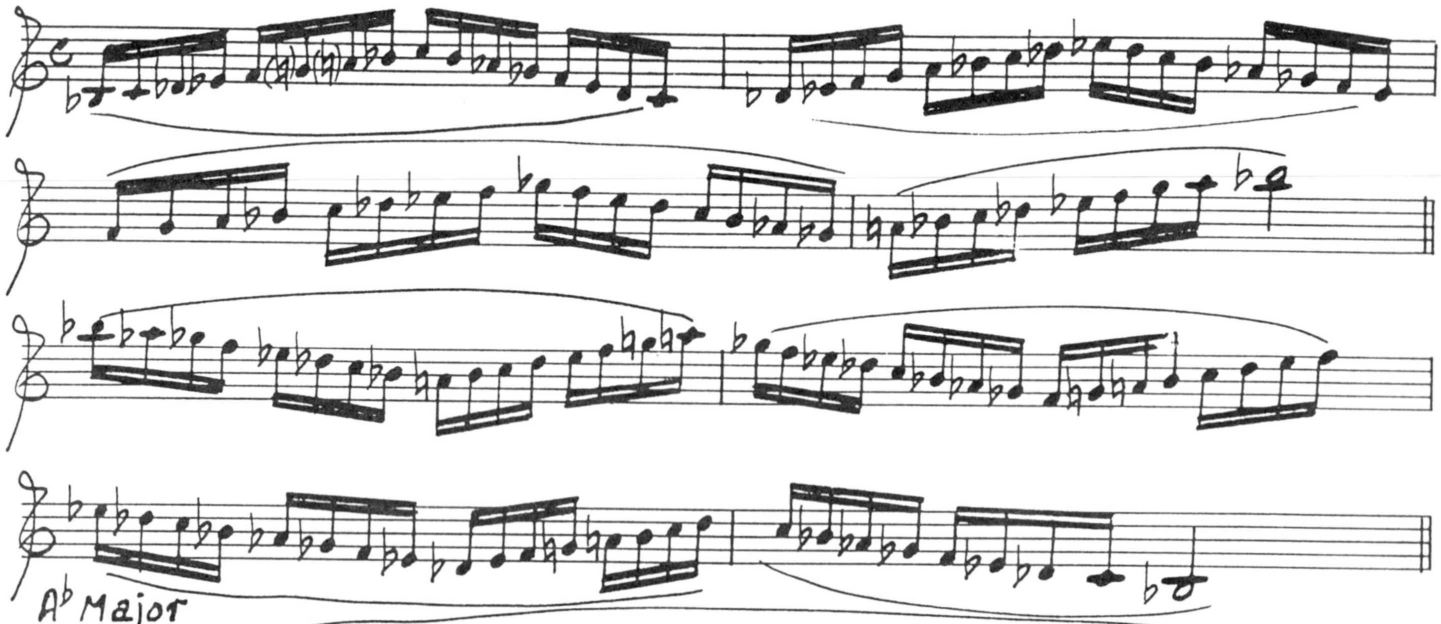

A♭ Major

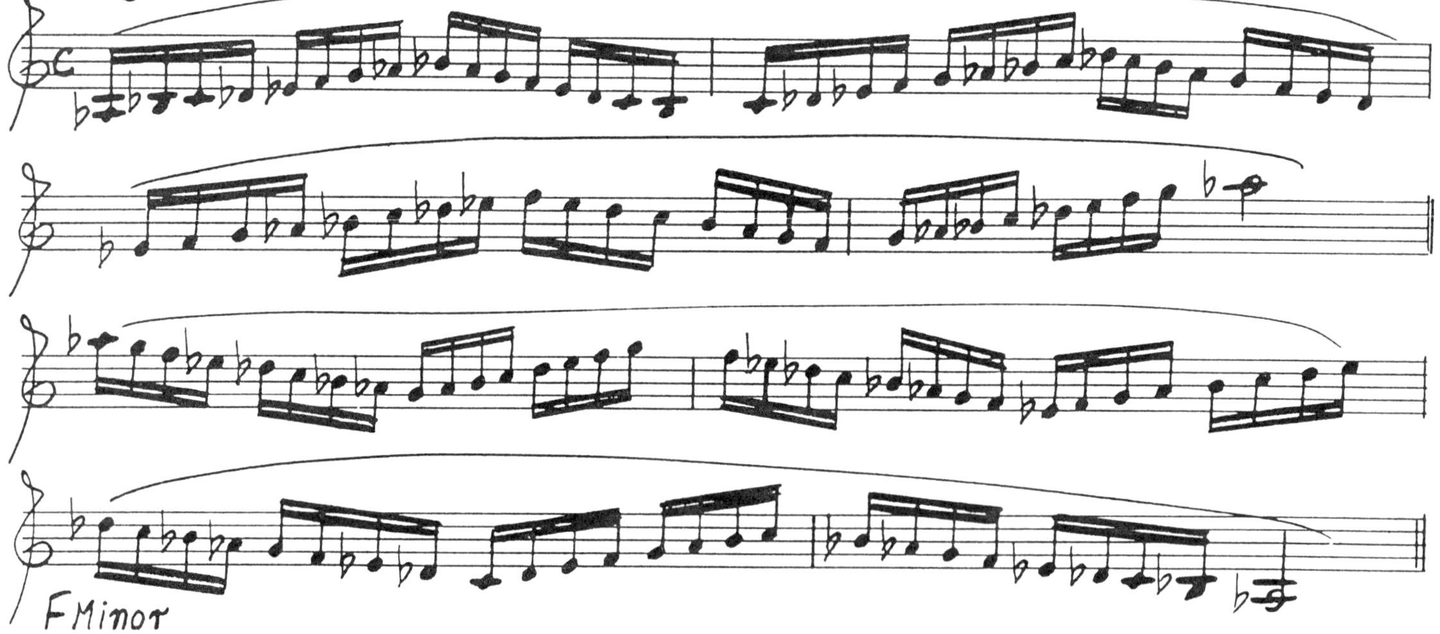

F Minor

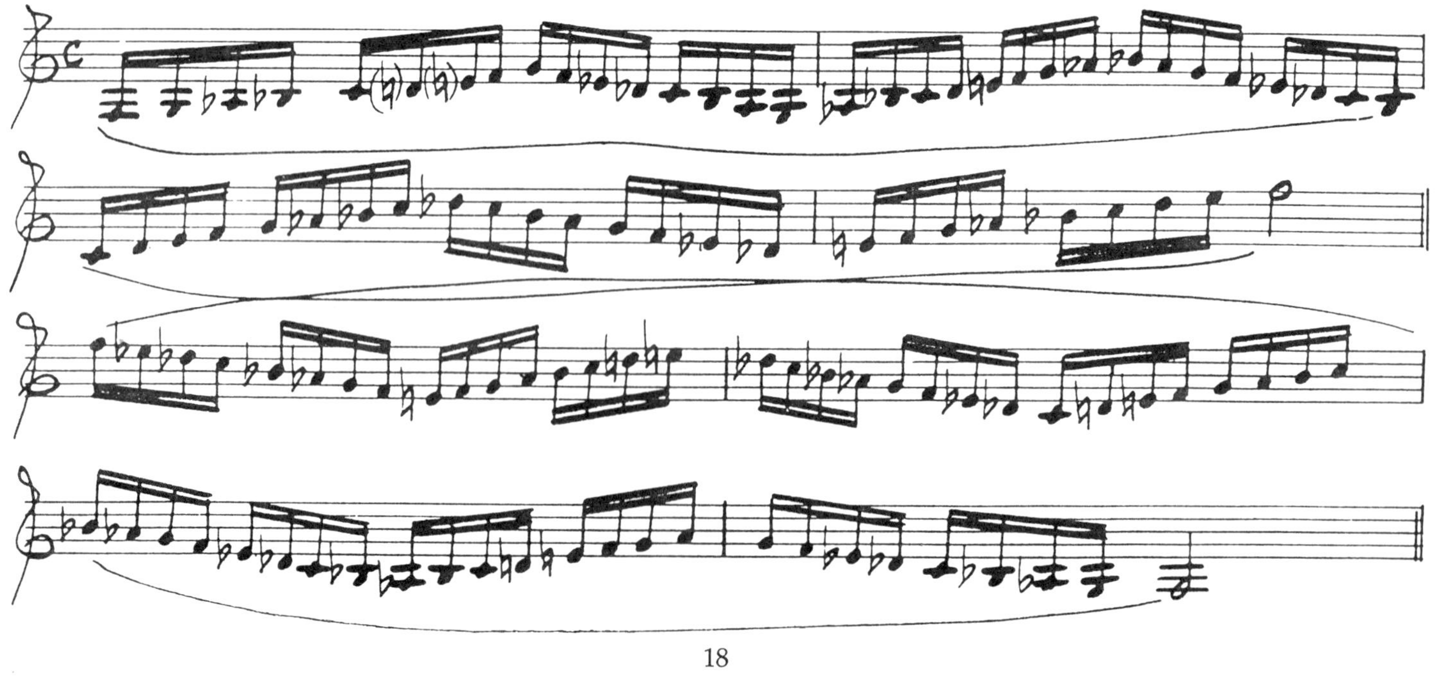

Eb Major

C Minor

Bb Major

G Minor

Scale record
5/27   126 bpm   OO 12-19

Section C

Chords

To accomplish our aims, in addition to acquiring a complete knowledge of scales (as treated in the previous section), we need also to be entirely at home with chords of all types. It is essential for you to become so skilled with chords that you can recognize by ear any chord played by another instrument, and reproduce the same chord on the clarinet, or construct a melodic passage based on that chord. Also, you should be able to produce any chord, given its name.

We will work with basic chords and also in the fields of altered chords, chord substitutions, chord extensions and polychordal devices. You will become familiar with basic chord progressions (the use of various chords one after another) and the process of developing substitute chord progressions to inject the modern jazz feeling into the music.

A chord consists of a group of three or more notes played simultaneously. There are many types of chords, the type depending upon the intervals between the component notes when these notes are arranged in their simplest position.

In the case of the clarinet and other instruments capable of playing only one note at a time, the nearest you can come to playing a chord is to play the chord notes one after another. This is called a broken chord, or arpeggio.

A chord containing only three essential notes is called a triad. In practical use, you frequently see one or more of the notes of a triad duplicated in a higher or lower octave. If a given note thus appears twice, we say it is "doubled."

Each chord has its foundation note, the note upon which the chord is constructed, called the "root" of the chord. The root is not necessarily the lowest note sounded. The lowest note sounded is called the "bass." Be sure you have a clear understanding of the difference between the root and the bass.

We will begin by showing the construction of the more common chords. For convenience, we will work with chords having the note C as the root. However, you must realize that any type of chord can be built on any root.

Each chord has a "symbol" which is an abbreviated description. A symbol consists of the letter name of the root plus information indicating the type of chord.

The "major" chord, being the simplest and most common of all, has as its symbol merely the letter name of the root— no other information. This chord is a triad and consists of the root plus a note a major third above the root (called the third of the chord), and a note a perfect fifth above the root (called the fifth of the chord).

Using only the notes of a C major scale, you can construct a total of three major chords—C major, F major, and G major.

When the root of any chord is in the bass (the lowest note sounded) we say that the chord is in root position. You will see, however, that not all root positions look exactly alike. If we rearrange the notes and put the third in the bass, the result is said to be in the first inversion. With the fifth in the bass, we have the second inversion.

These C major chords are all in root position.

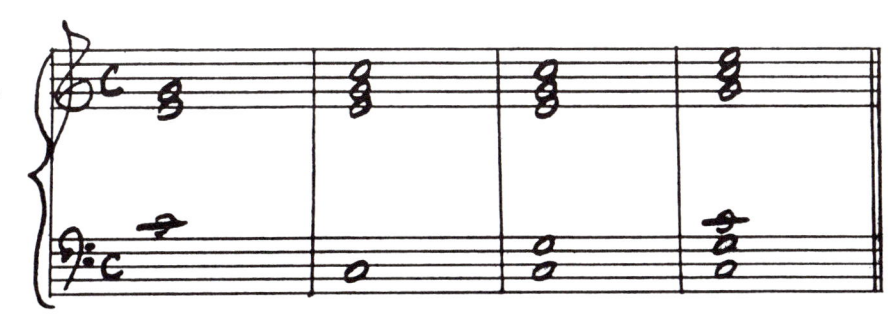

These are in the first inversion.   These are in the second inversion.

Chords consisting basically of four notes can also have a third inversion. Those with five notes can have a fourth inversion, et

A "minor" chord, indicated by a symbol consisting of the letter name of the root followed by a small mi, consists of the roo
a minor third, and a perfect fifth.

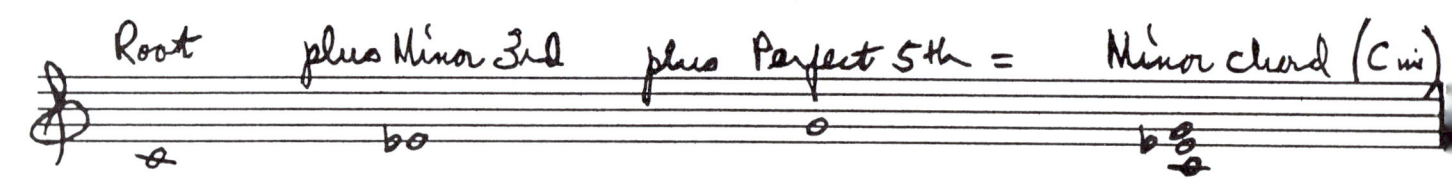

Root   plus Minor 3rd   plus Perfect 5th =   Minor chord (Cmi)

Using only the notes of a C major scale, you can construct a total of three minor chords—Dmi, Emi, and Ami.

A "dominant seventh" chord (frequently called simply a "seventh" chord) is indicated by the root and the number 7.
It consists of a major chord plus a note a minor seventh above the root.

Major chord   plus Minor 7th = Dominant 7th chord (C7)

Using only the notes of a C major scale, you can construct only one dominant seventh chord—G7. Notice that G is the fifth
degree, or dominant, in the C major scale, hence the name of the chord.

If you raise or lower one or more of the notes in a chord, the resulting chord is said to be "altered." Many altered chords
are used in both traditional harmony and in modern jazz harmony.

An "augmented" or "augmented fifth" chord results when you alter a major chord by raising its fifth a half-step. The symbol is the root and a plus sign.

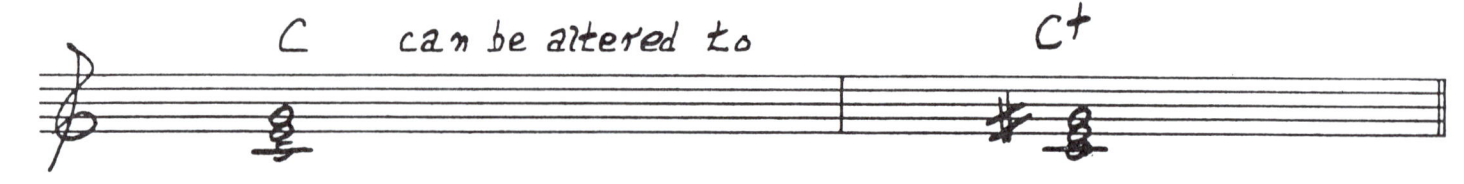

C   can be altered to   C+

A more complex alteration results when you lower the third, fifth, and seventh of a dominant seventh chord to produce a "diminished seventh" chord, usually called simply a "diminished" chord. The symbol is the root and the abbreviation "dim." Or—

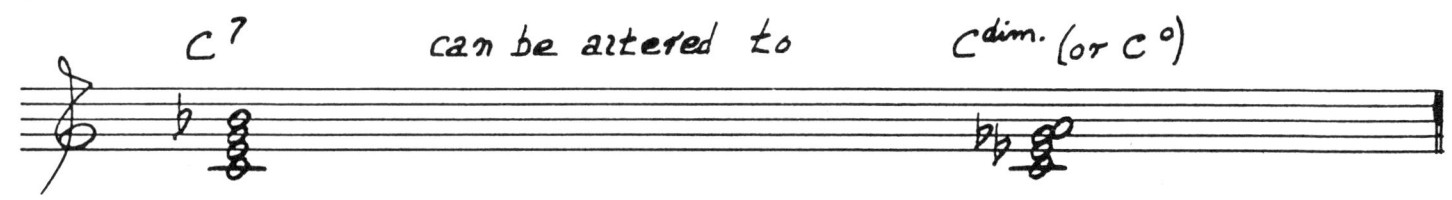

The name of this chord suggests that when properly spelled out, the interval between the root and the highest note should be a diminished seventh, which would be C to Bbb (B-double-flat). Using A as the top note instead is rather common because it has been found to be practical. You will frequently find the Gb appearing as F#.

Next we have some exercises in which the chords discussed appear in arpeggio form. Play these to get familiar with the sound and the feel of these chords.

Some chords have a strong tendency to move (resolve) to certain other chords in order to satisfy the ear. A dominant seventh chord having as its root the dominant (V) of a key tends to resolve to a major chord the root of which is the tonic (I) of that key. For example, G7 resolves to C; C7 resolves to F; D7 resolves to G, etc. This information may also be expressed thus: a dominant seventh chord has as its root the fifth of the major chord to which it resolves. Here is an example.

To give you some practice with this procedure, we now have written exercises in the form of tests.

TEST A. Write in the notes and symbol of the major chord to which each of these dominant seventh chords should resolve. Answers on next page.

Now we will show an arpeggio based on the dominant seventh chord in one measure, and in the next we show an arpeggio based on the major chord to which it resolves.

TEST B. In a manner similar to the above example, write in each blank measure an arpeggio type of passage based on the major chord to which each dominant seventh chord resolves. Give the chord symbol in each case. Answers on next page.

Answers to TEST A on previous page.

Answers to TEST B on previous page. After you study these and compare them with your answers, play over the music to get the sound and feel.

Now we will acquaint you with the name, construction, and symbol of a good many additional chords. As before, they will be shown for explanatory purposes with the note C as the root. In each case the component notes are first shown grouped in chord form, then shown as an arpeggio. The arpeggios should be played over on the instrument to help you to learn the sound and get the feel of each chord. All of this material must be studied carefully, then used for reference.

To a major chord add a note a major sixth above the root and you have a major sixth chord, usually called simply a sixth chord.

To a minor chord add a note a major sixth above the root and you have a minor sixth chord.

A minor chord plus a note a minor seventh above the root gives a minor seventh chord.

A major chord plus a note a major seventh above the root gives a major seventh chord.

When a dominant seventh chord is altered by raising the fifth of the chord a half-step, the result is a dominant seventh augmented fifth chord.

By lowering the fifth of a dominant seventh chord a half-step you form a dominant seventh diminished fifth chord.

By lowering the fifth of a minor seventh chord a half-step you form a minor seventh diminished fifth chord.

By adding higher notes to some of the chords we already know, we can construct chords having a top note more than an octave above the root. This procedure, called extending the chords, is of prime importance in modern jazz, since the extended chords or upper structure triads give a modern sound and supply additional material for use in improvising a modern jazz line. There are a great many possibilities in the area of altered and extended chords. We will deal with the more important ones.

A sixth chord can be extended to form a sixth add ninth chord.

A minor sixth chord can be extended to form a minor sixth add ninth chord.

A minor seventh chord can be extended to form a minor seventh add ninth chord.

A seventh chord can be extended to form a ninth chord.

A seventh chord can be extended to form a seventh add augmented ninth chord, or raised ninth.

A seventh chord can be extended to form a seventh add minor ninth chord, frequently called simply a minor ninth chord.

A seventh augmented fifth chord can be extended to form a ninth augmented fifth chord.

A seventh augmented fifth chord can be extended to form a seventh augmented fifth add minor ninth chord.

A seventh diminished fifth chord can be extended to form a ninth diminished fifth chord.

A major seventh chord can be extended to form a major seventh add ninth chord.

A ninth chord can be extended to an eleventh chord.	C¹¹
A ninth chord can be extended to an augmented eleventh chord.	C Aug.¹¹ or C⁹⁺¹¹
A ninth chord can be extended to a thirteenth chord.	C¹³
A ninth chord can be extended to an eleventh add thirteenth chord (a thirteenth chord in which the eleventh is present).	C¹¹⁽¹³⁾
A ninth chord can be extended to an augmented eleventh add thirteenth chord.	C Aug.¹¹⁽¹³⁾ or C¹³⁺¹¹
A minor ninth chord can be extended to an augmented eleventh minor ninth add thirteenth chord.	C¹¹⁻⁹⁽¹³⁾ or C¹³⁻⁹₊₁₁
A minor ninth chord can be extended to a thirteenth minor ninth chord.	C¹³⁻⁹
A minor ninth chord can be extended to a minor ninth add minor thirteenth chord.	C⁷⁻⁹⁻¹³

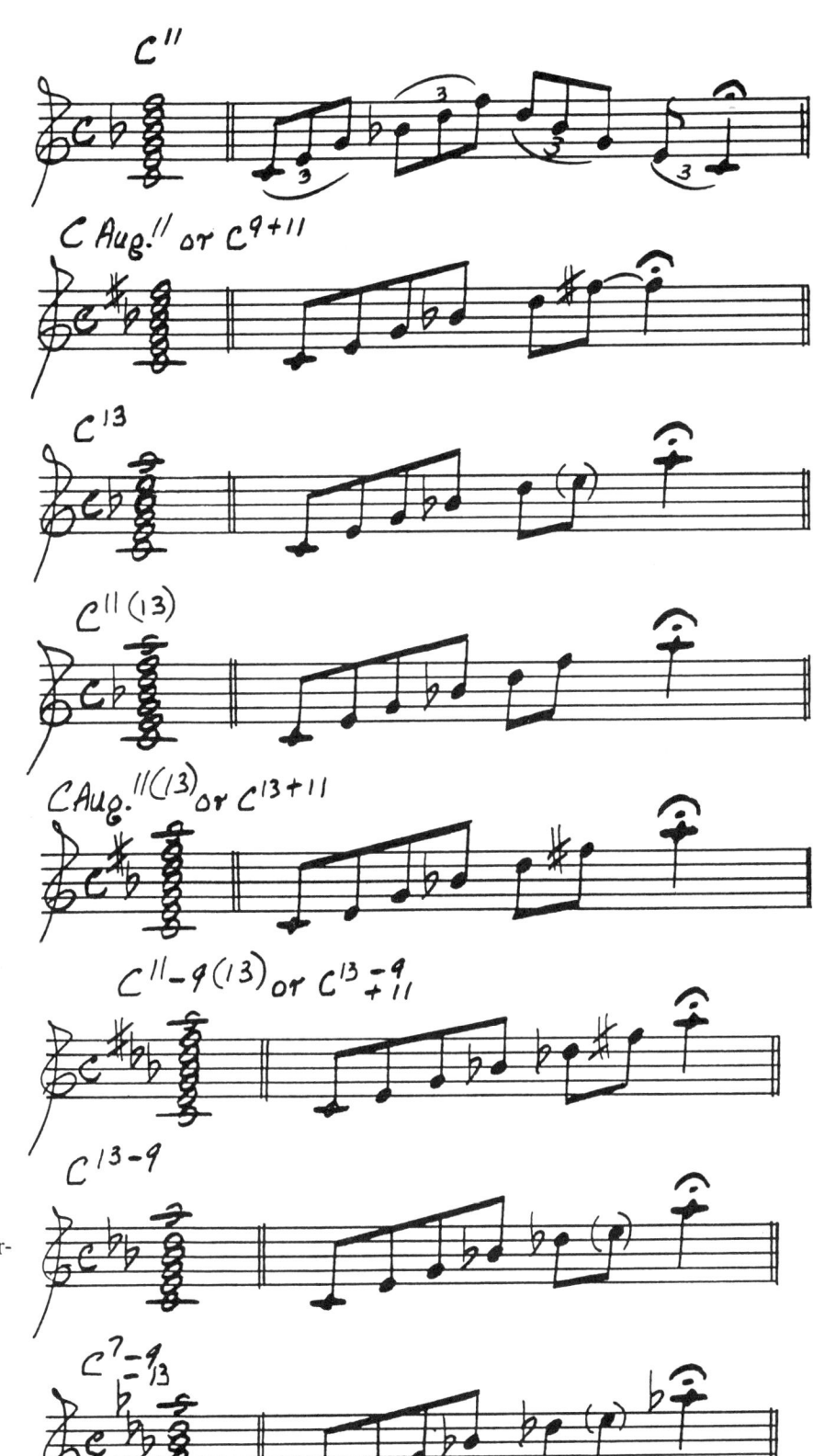

Indicating the structure of chords by means of chord symbols is by no means standardized. There is considerable disagreement among musicians on this subject. One musician will show a chord with a certain symbol; another musician will show the same chord with a somewhat different symbol. Here are some of the equivalents.

C+ = C aug.
C dim. = C°
C7+5 = C7#5 = C7+

C7-5 = C7b5 = C7-
C7-9 = C7(b9) = C-9

C⁹/₆ = C⁹/6 = C6(9)
Cm⁹/₆ = Cm⁹/6 = Cm6(9)

C aug. 11 = C+11 = C11+
C13-9 = C13(b9)
C aug. 11 (13 = C+11 (13) = C11+ (13)

C7-9 (-13) = C7-9 (b13) = C⁻¹³₋₉
Cmi (bass) = A-7b5

29

A dominant seventh chord, or an alteration or extension of it, has a tendency to resolve to a major chord whose root is a perfect fifth lower or a perfect fourth higher. In modern jazz the major chord can (and should) be present as a substitute or extension, such as a sixth chord, a major seventh chord, a sixth add ninth chord, or one of many others. The selection of the particular chord to which the resolution is made is dictated largely by the individual's ear, taste, and concept.

Here are some examples of typical resolutions. Study the chords and play them as presented in arpeggio form to get the sound and feel of these resolutions.

Rhythm

The Jazz rhythm factor is so varied and ambiguous that alone, it would require too much time and space here. Moreover, the "actual" idea of "swing" cannot be absolutely described with words and charts.

One must "experience" swing (Jazz feel) by playing and listening first hand on the physical-emotional eg: "somatic" level. However, I would recommend playing with a metronome to establish steady, even rhythm.

Additional Daily Scale Studies

Scales

At this point we will introduce some scale studies that should be added to your daily routine of technical material.

The half-diminished scale was nothing new to the modern symphonic composers, but it was only during the early "forties" when they were introduced into modern jazz. Since then they have become standard in jazz.

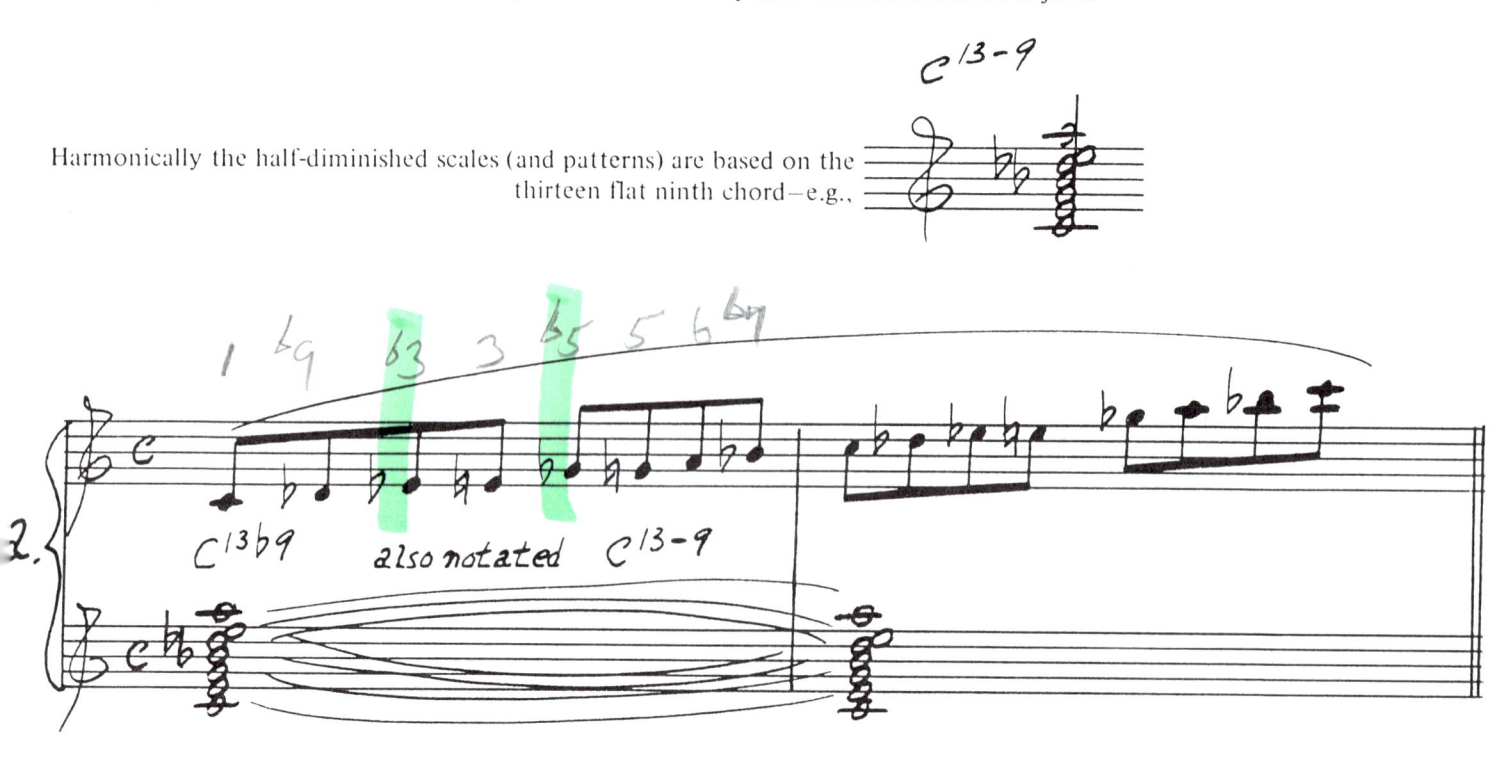

Harmonically the half-diminished scales (and patterns) are based on the thirteen flat ninth chord – e.g., C^{13-9}

b. E♭13-9

c. G♭13-9

d. A13-9

Enharmonically, the above scale can be written; etc.

35

There are four half-diminished scales for each of the three diminished chords or tonalities.

The following are some examples and also some variations on these basic scales—

Half-diminished scale patterns

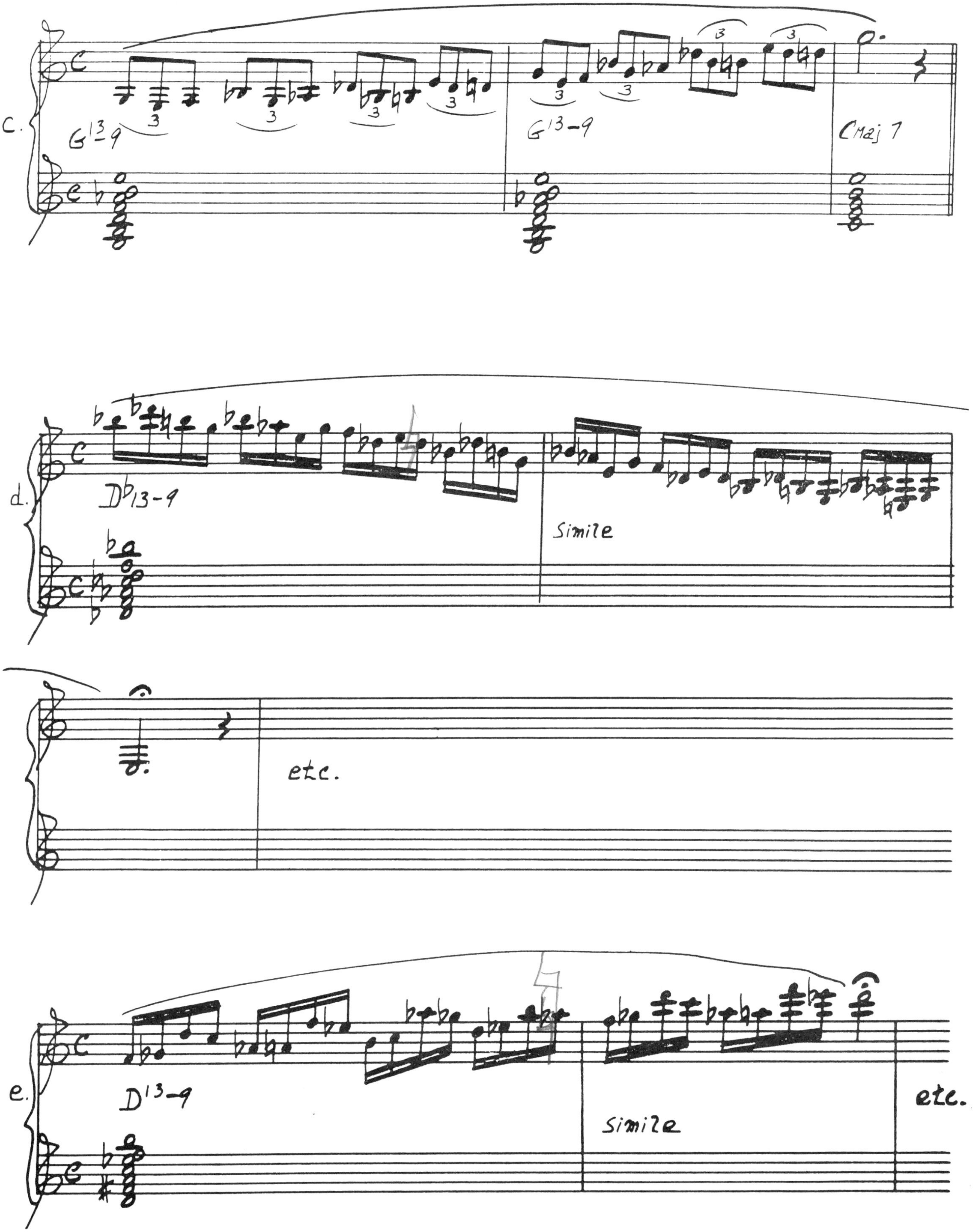
c.
G13-9
G13-9
CMaj 7
d.
D♭13-9
simile
etc.
e.
D13-9
simile
etc.

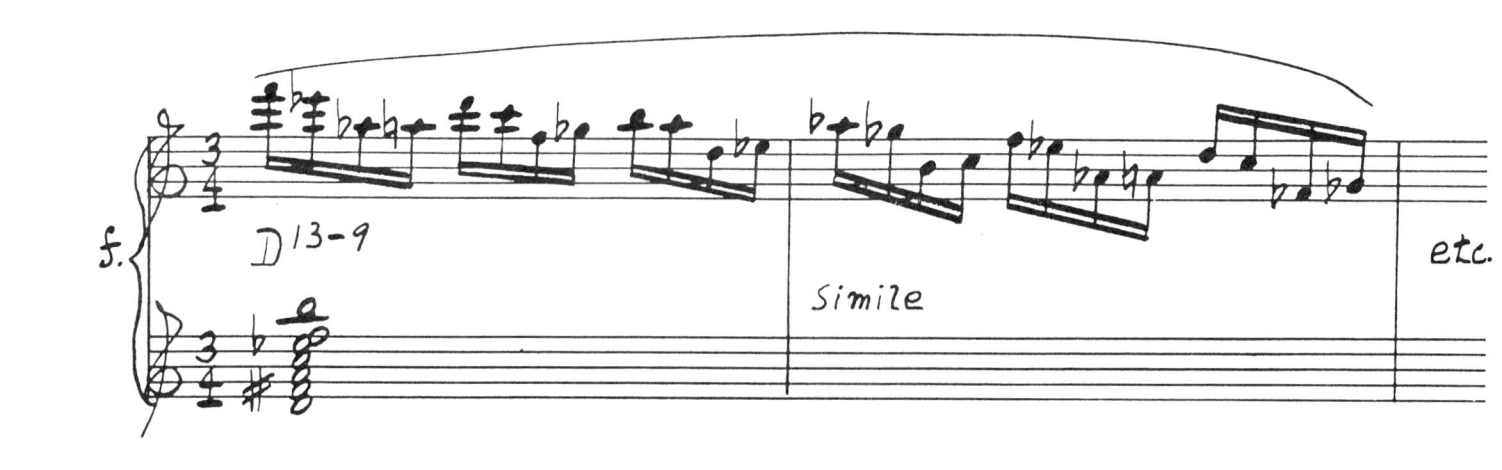

Half-diminished studies cont'd.

Tommy Dorsey used to like these!!

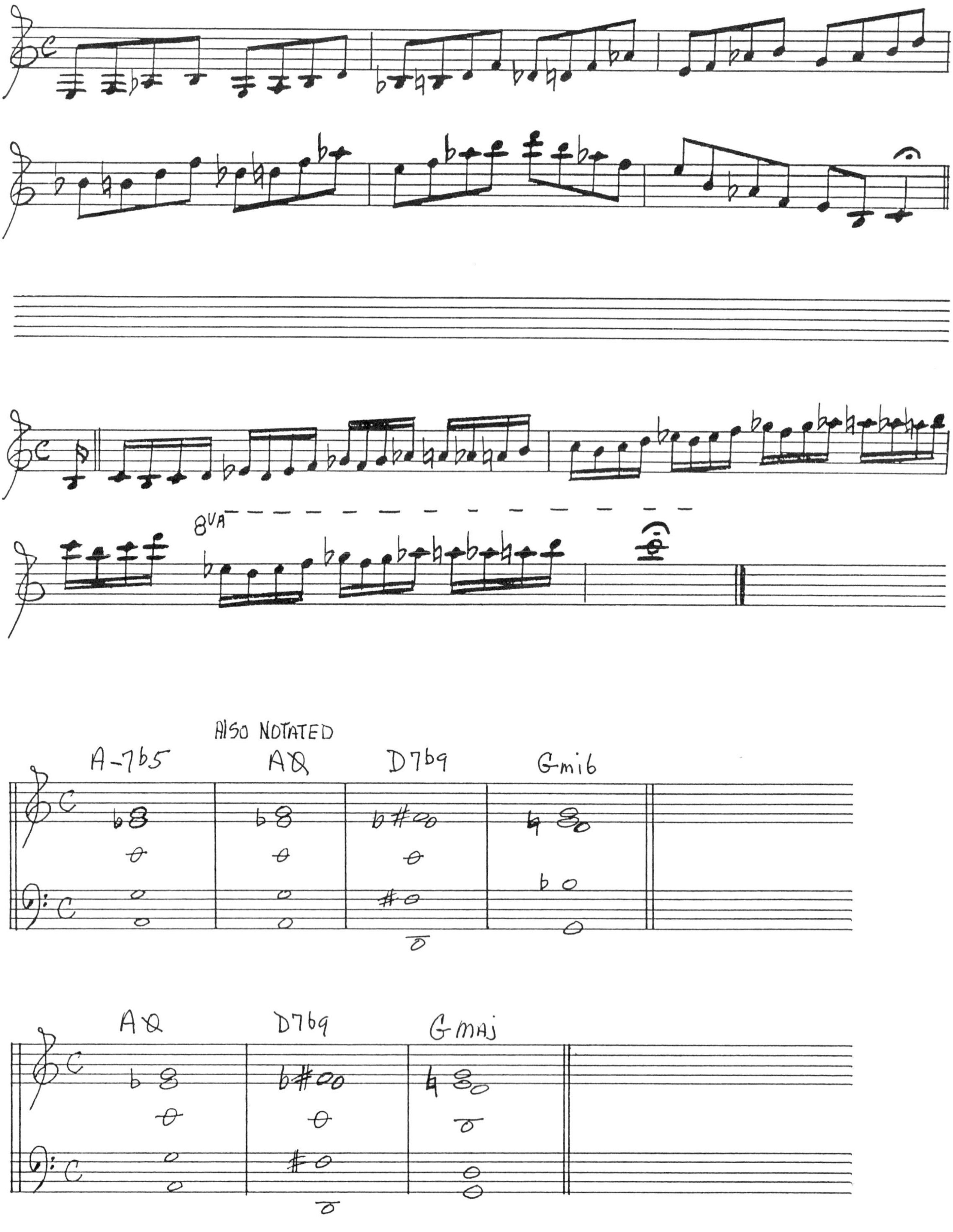

8VA
ALSO NOTATED
A-7b5
Aø
D7b9
Gmi6
Aø
D7b9
G MAJ

Section D

Here, we arrive at my "Hanon" phase of this book.

I believe that when you play these exercises, in "all keys" as indicated, you can develop your technique to enable you to play, pretty much, what comes into your mind with relative ease.

Note: it is good "practice" to accent the first note of patterns of 4

as in: [musical example]

however, do not carry this into your professional playing unless indicated on your part.

> **The Hanon exercises should be practiced as follows:**
> 1. All of exercise 1, all of 2, all of 3, all of 4.
> 2. All of exercise 4, all of 5, all of 6, all of 7.
> 3. All of exercise 7, all of 8, all of 9, all of 10.
> 4. All of exercise 10, all of 11, all of 12, all of 13.
> 5. All of exercise 13, all of 14, all of 15, all of 16.
> 6. All of exercise 16, all of 17, all of 18, all of 19 & 20.

Ex. 1

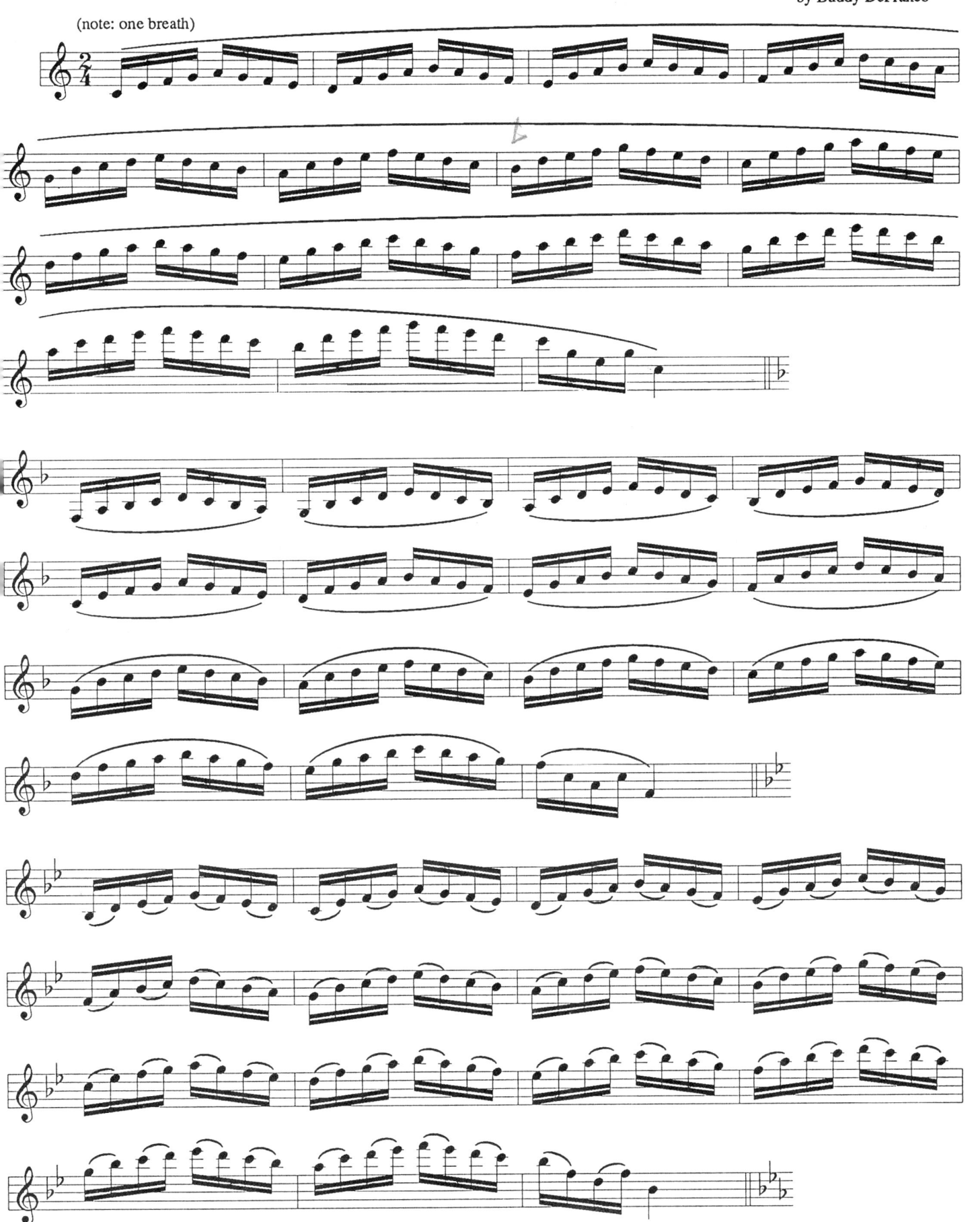

Hanon Exercises
Transcribed for clarinet
by Buddy DeFranco

(note: one breath)

(Ex. 1)

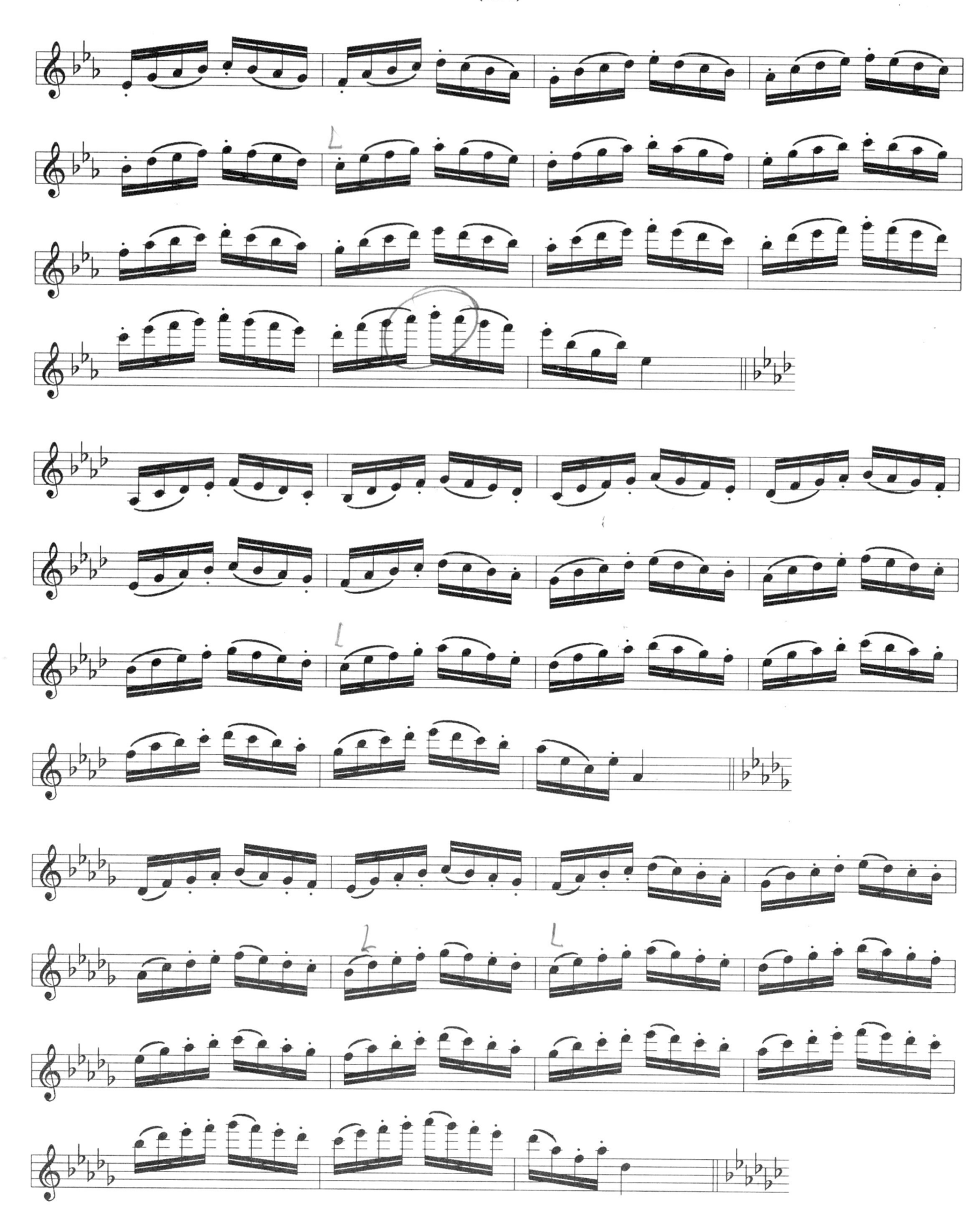

(Ex. 1)

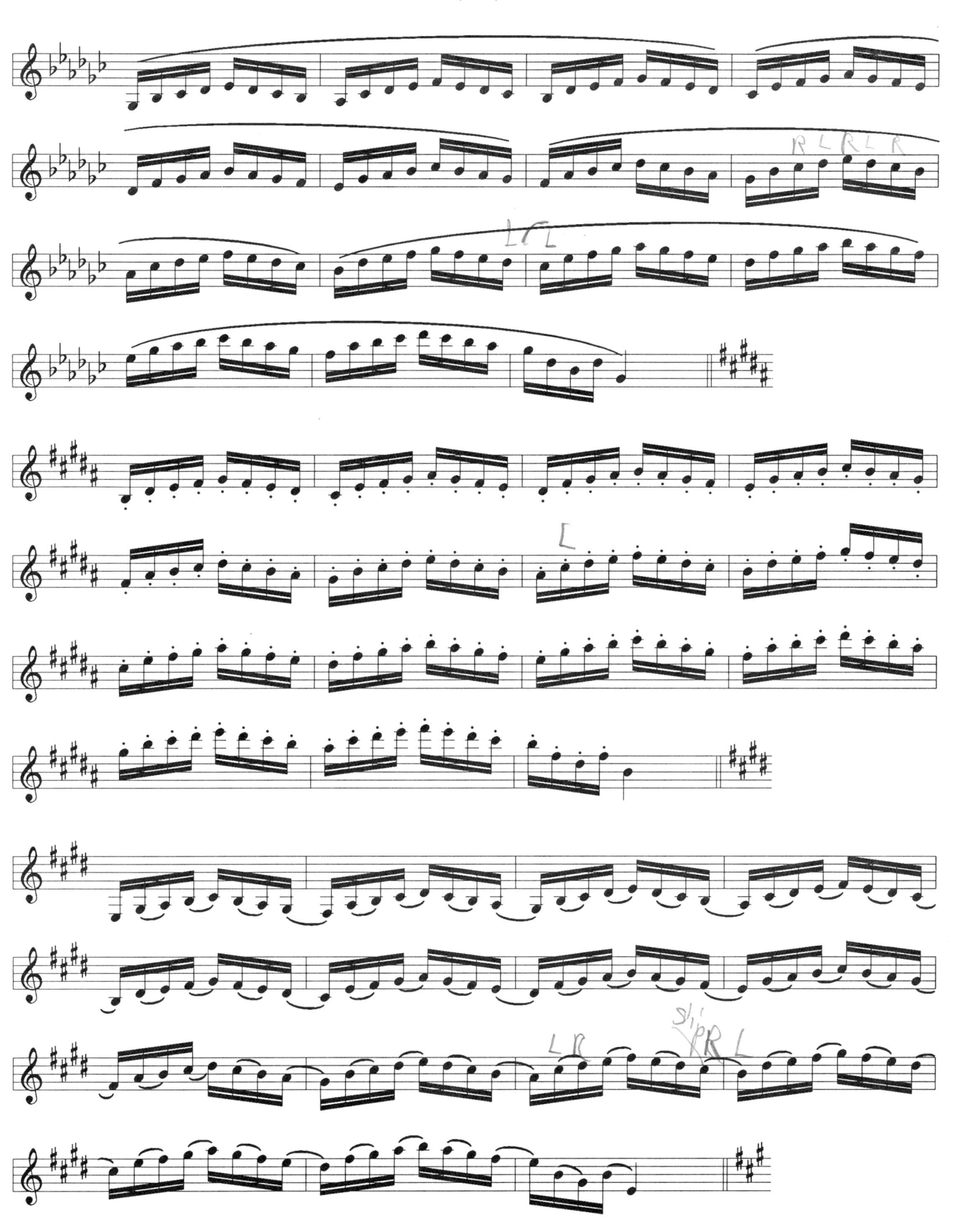

(Ex. 1)

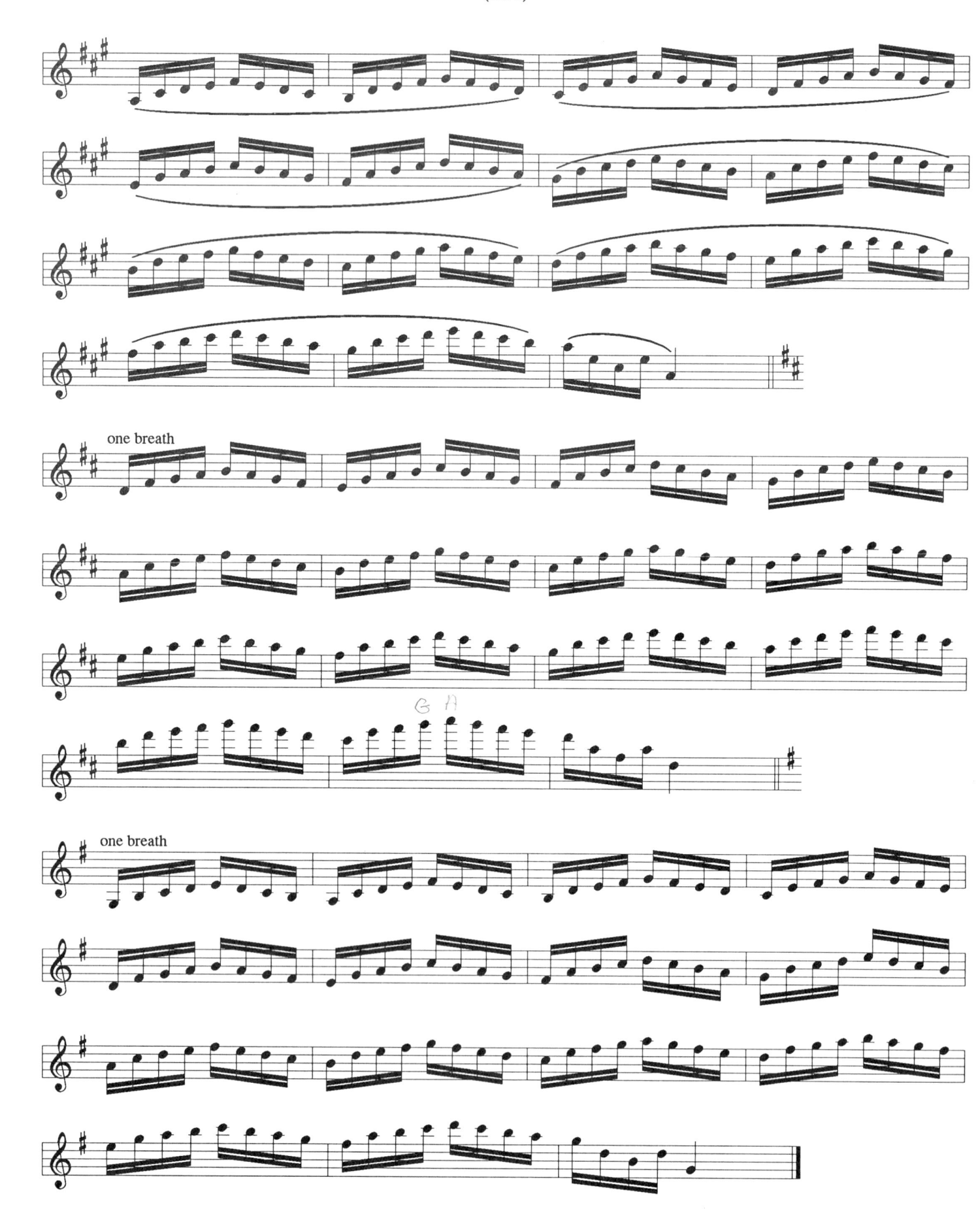

Ex. 2

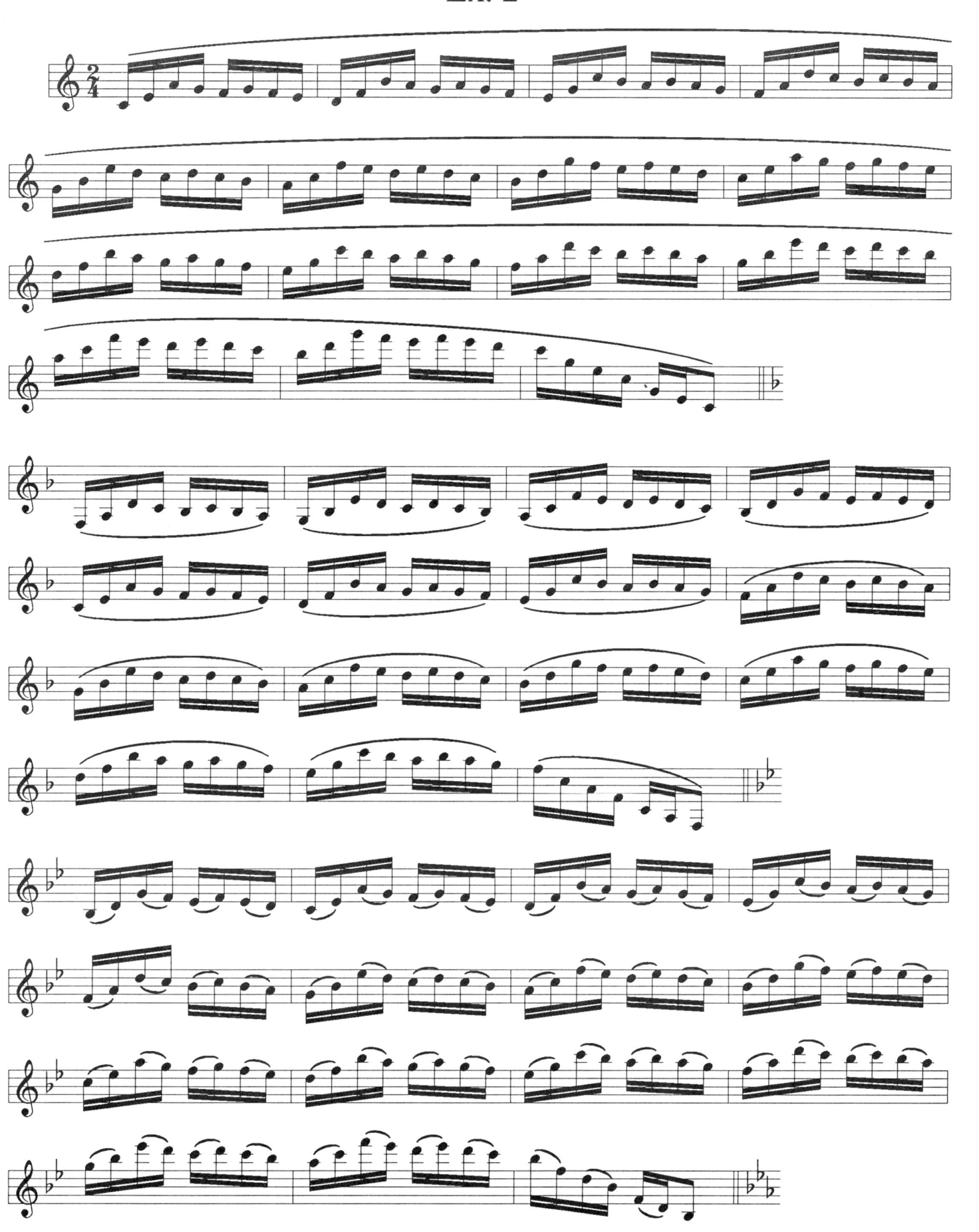

(Ex. 2)

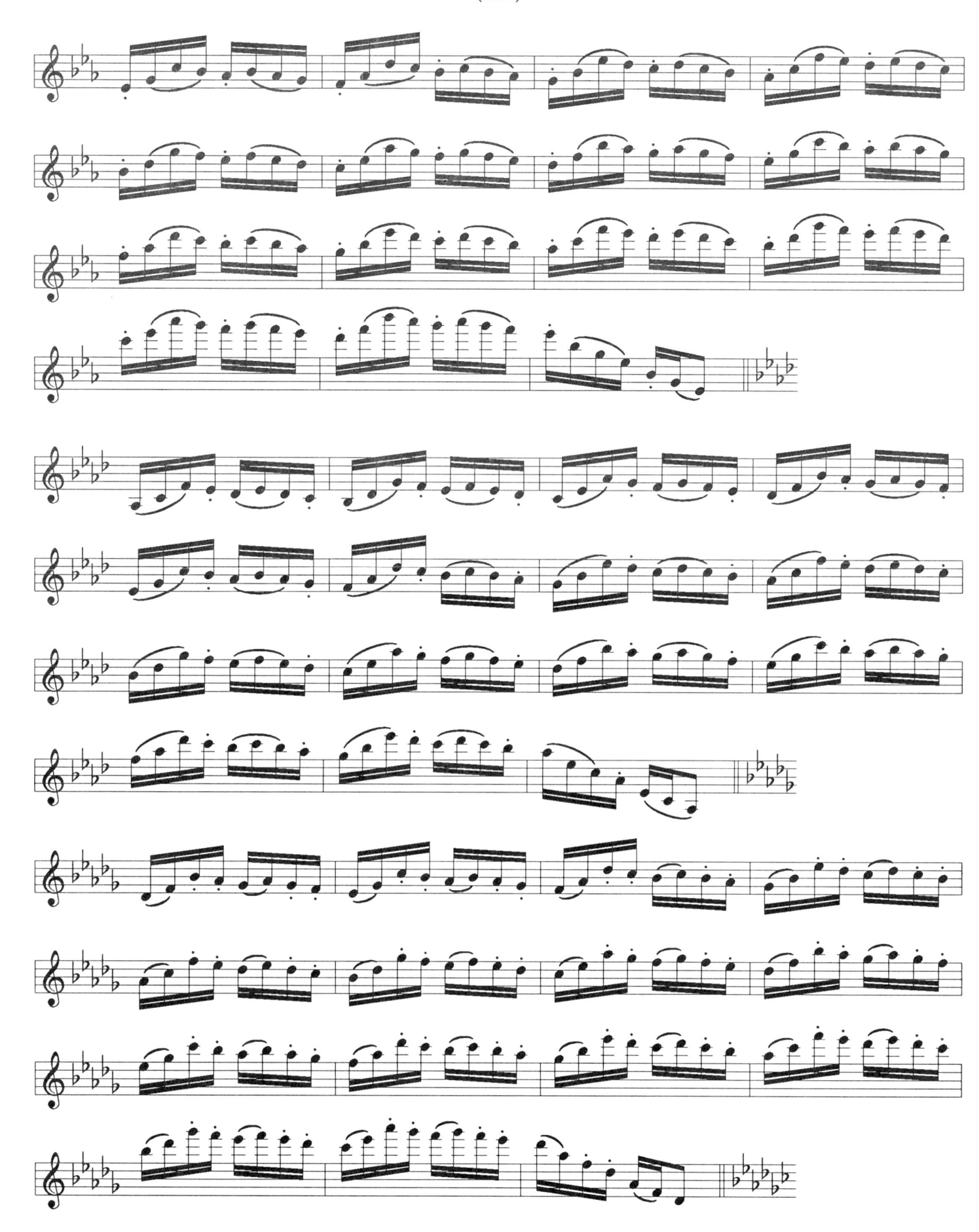

(Ex. 2)

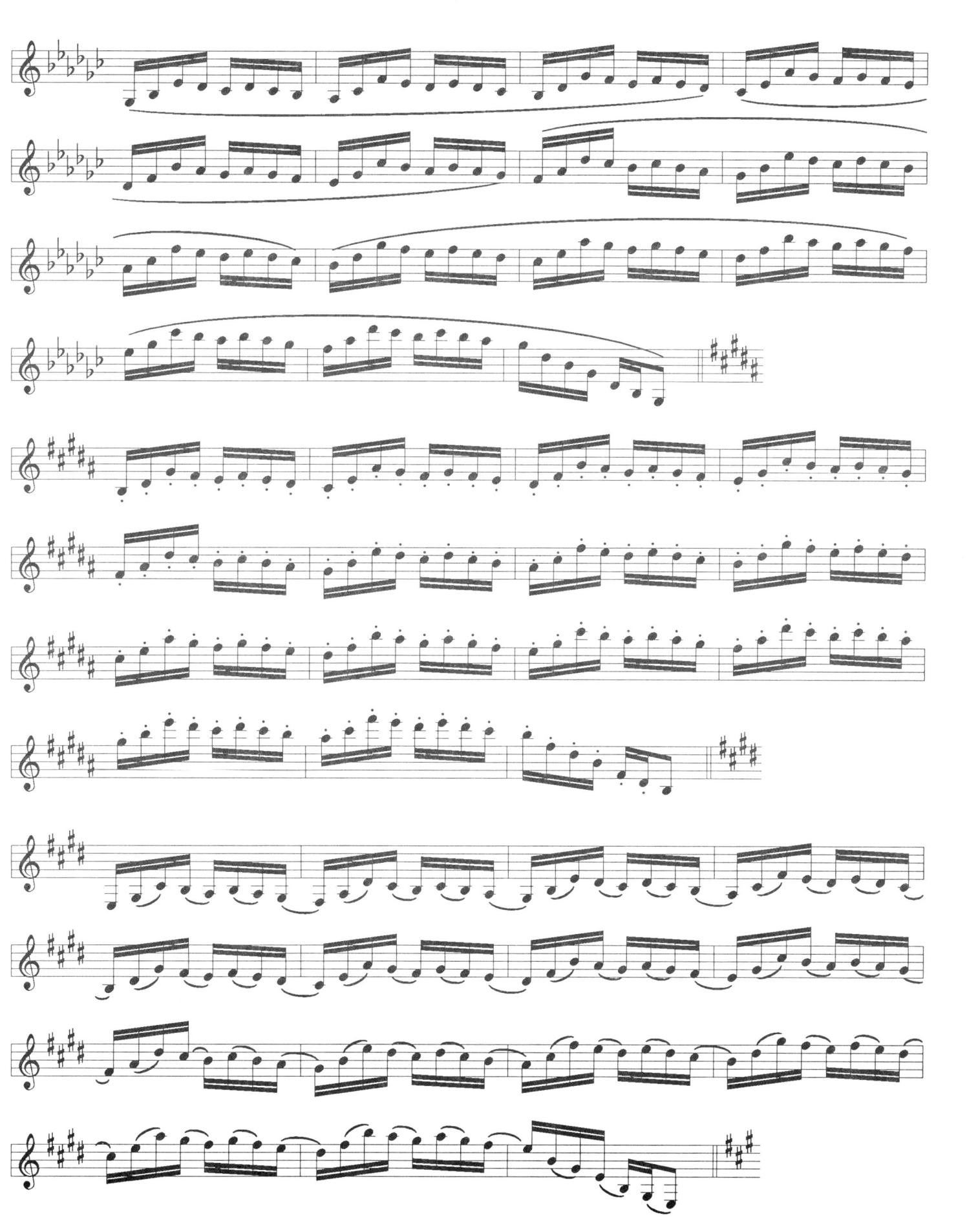

(Ex. 2)

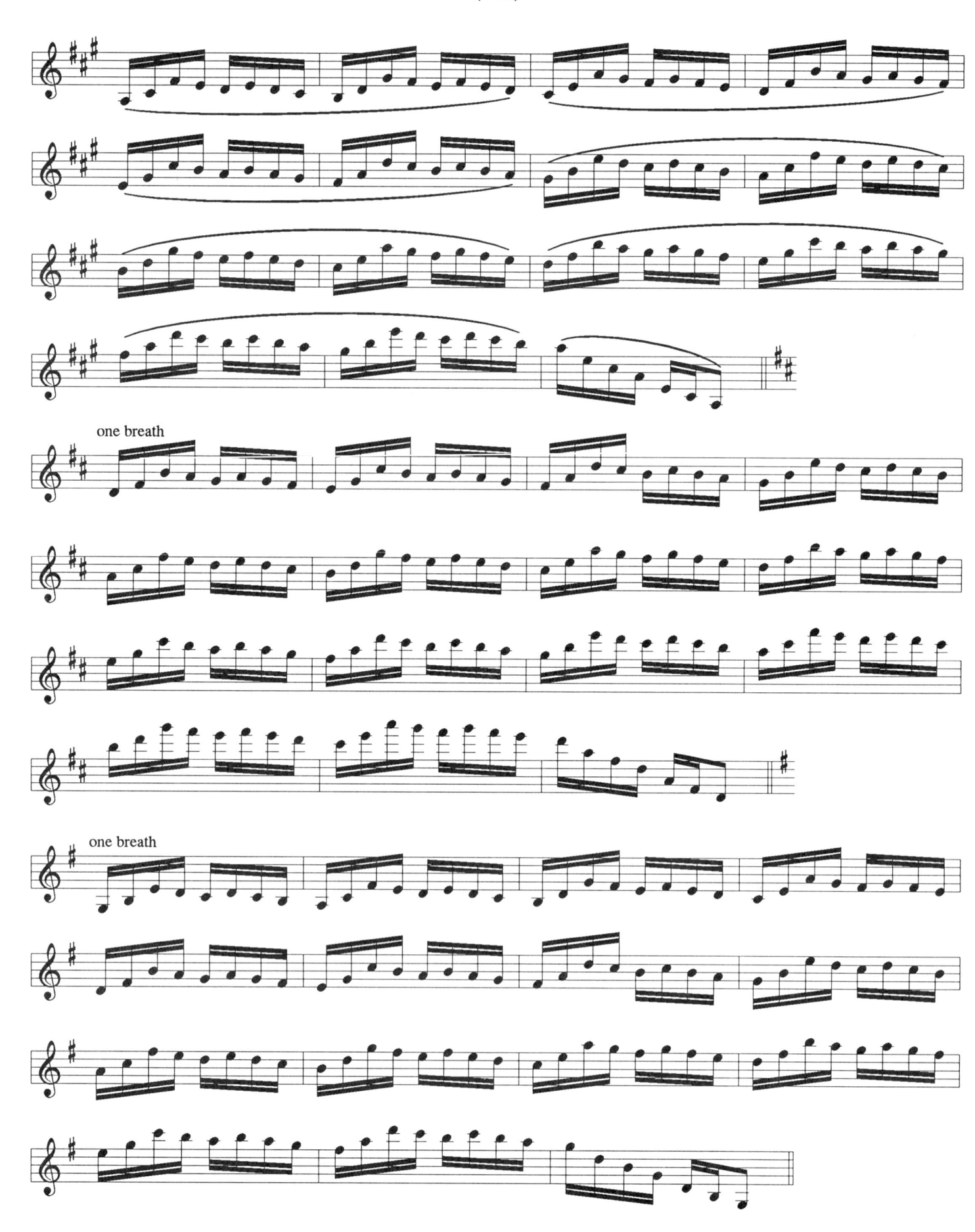

Ex. 3

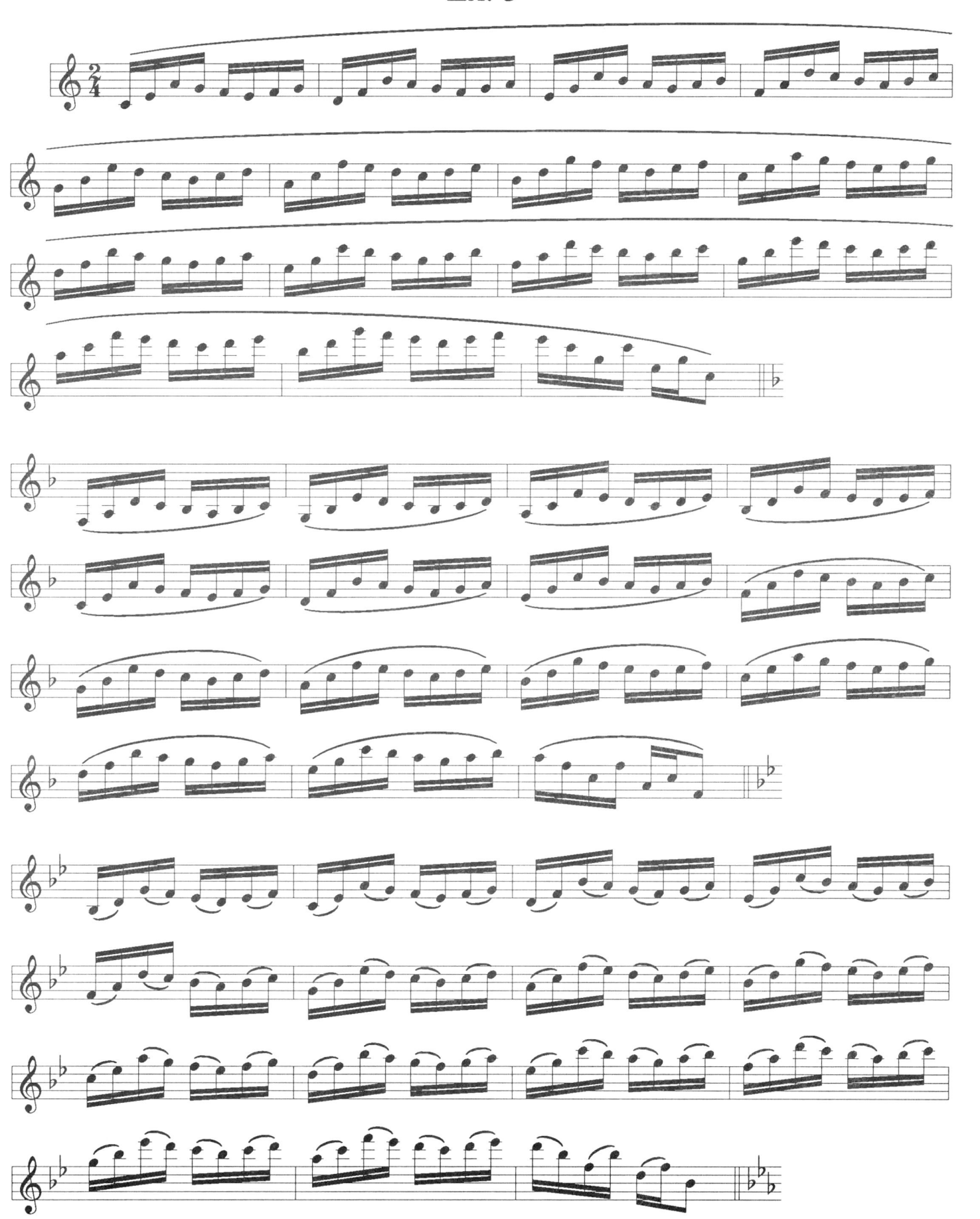

(Ex. 3)

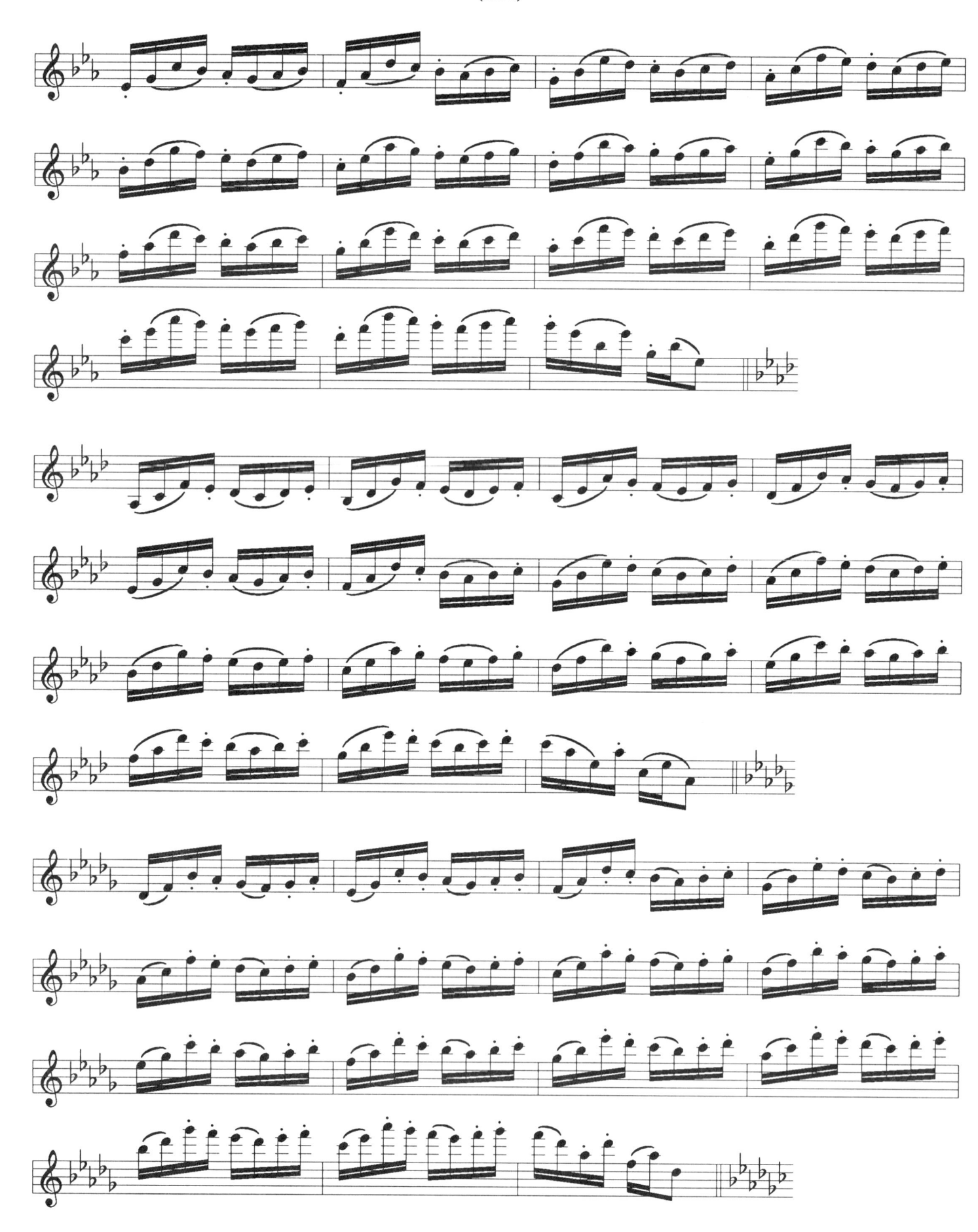

(Ex. 3)

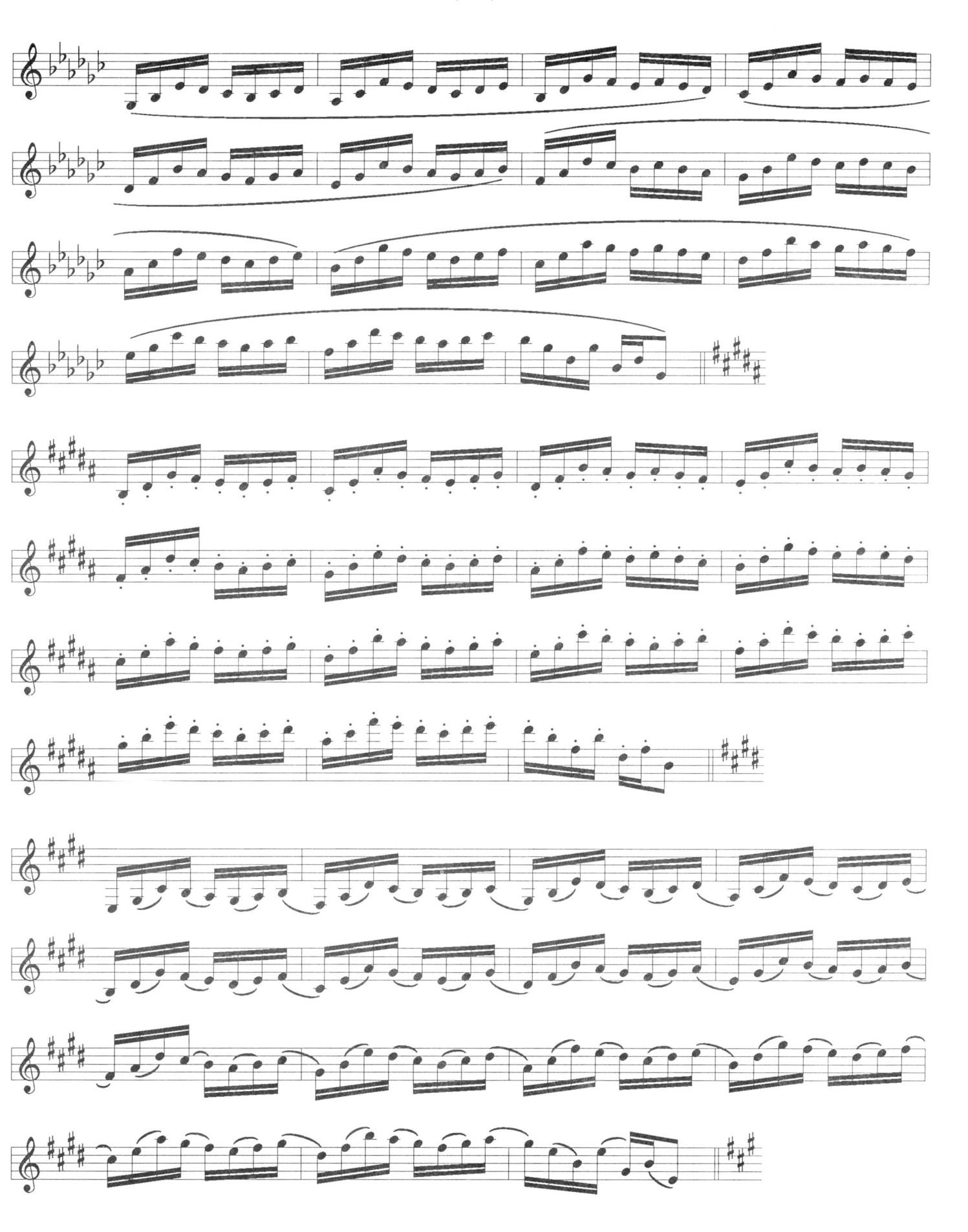

(Ex. 3)

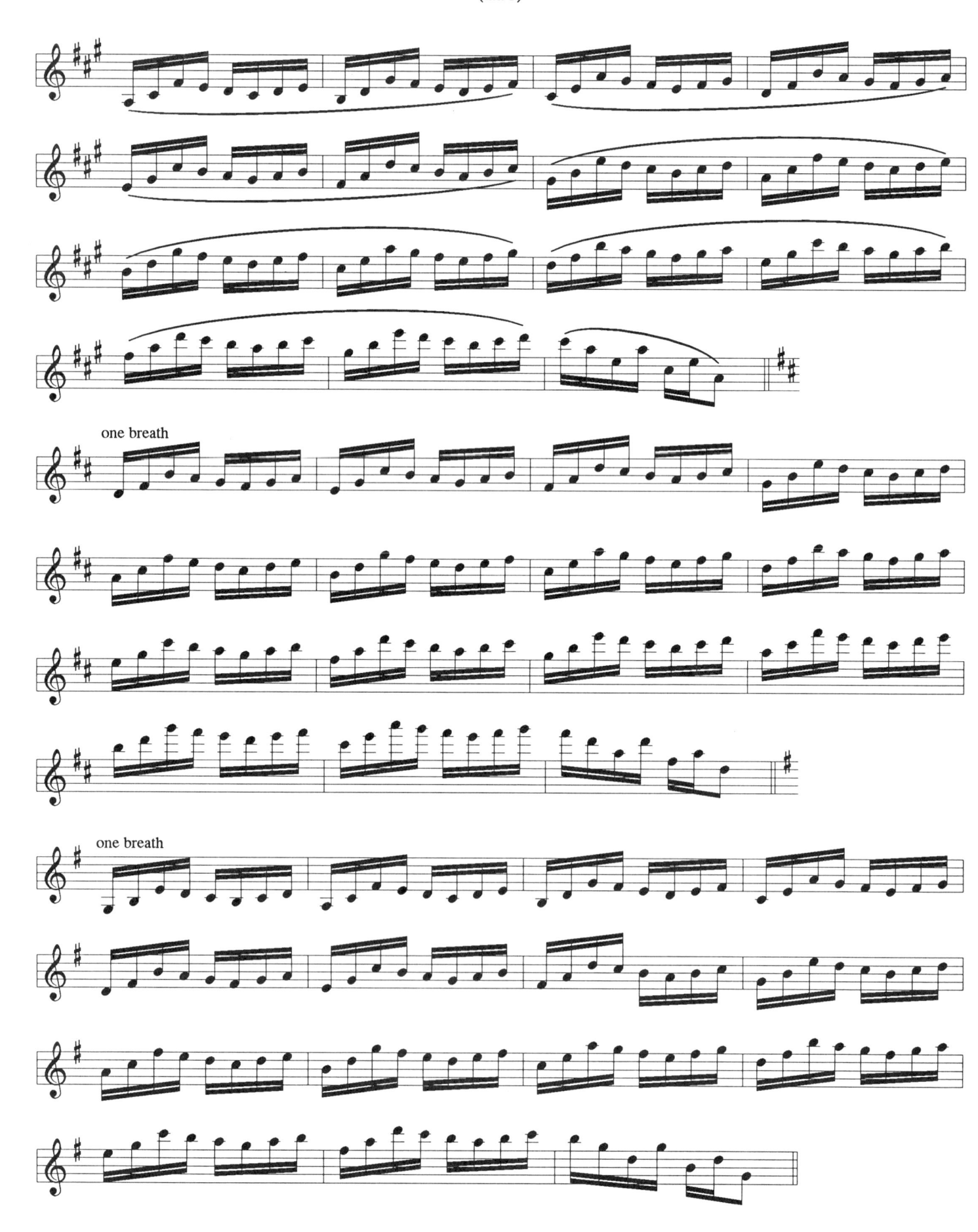

Ex. 4

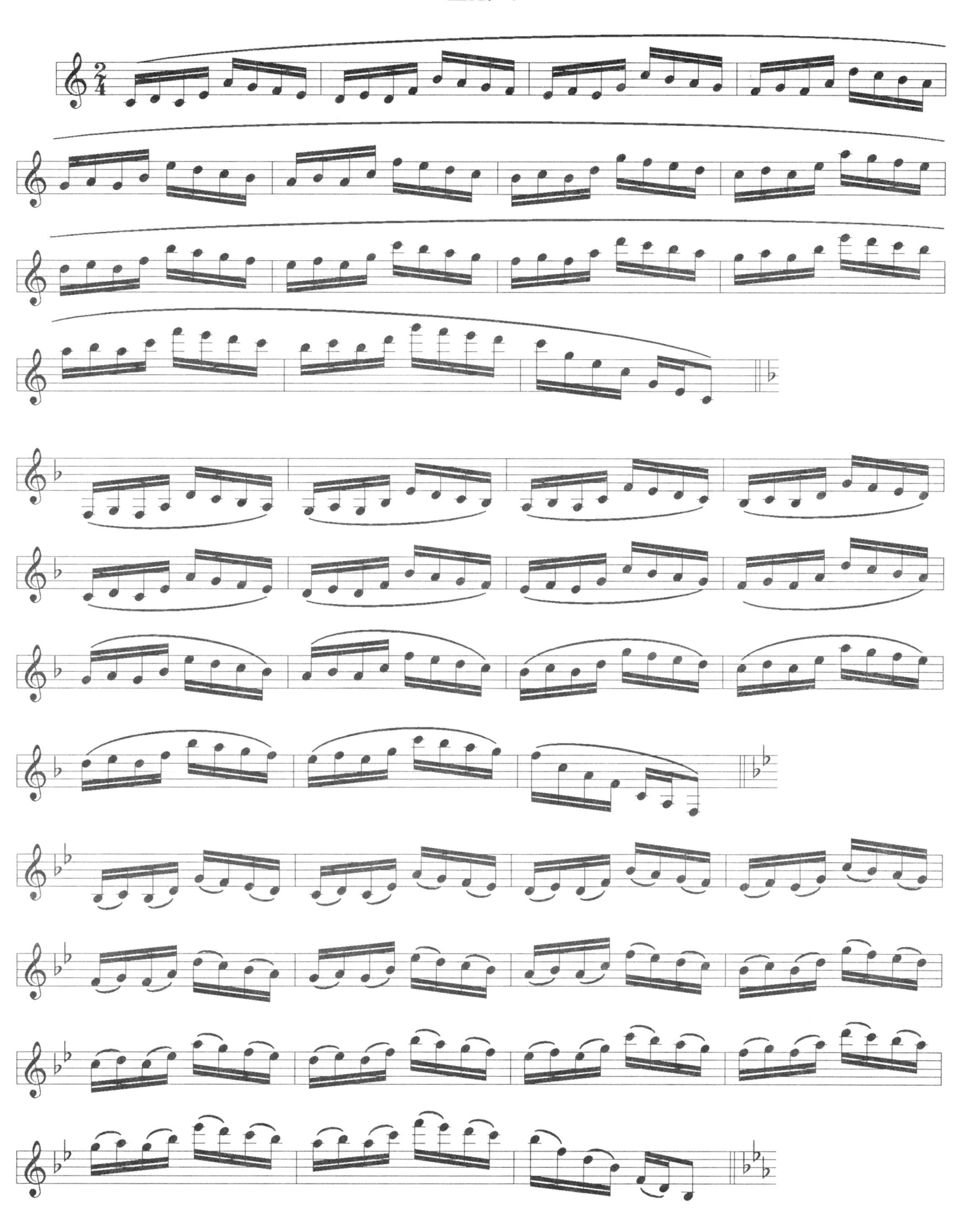

(Ex. 4)

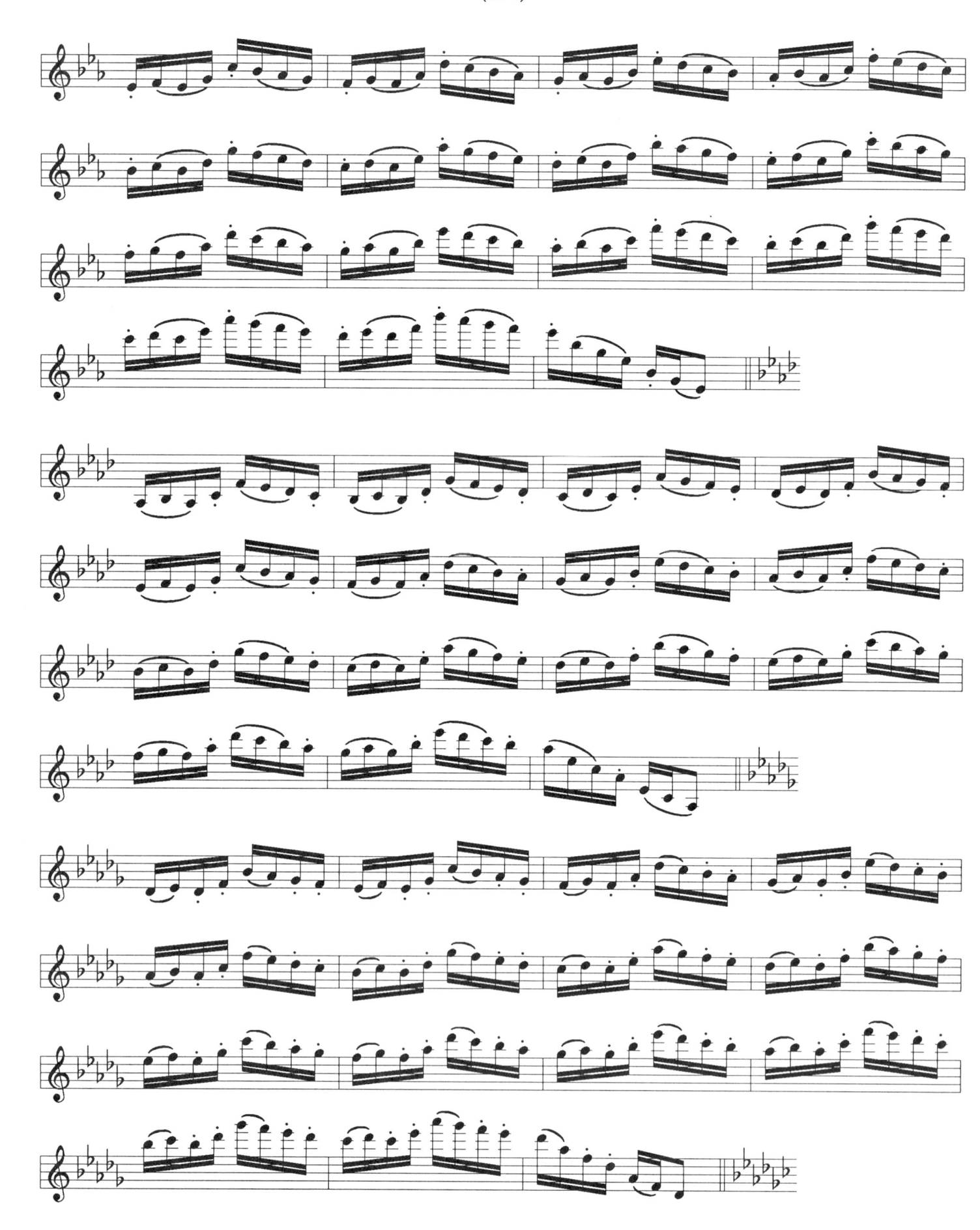

(Ex. 4)

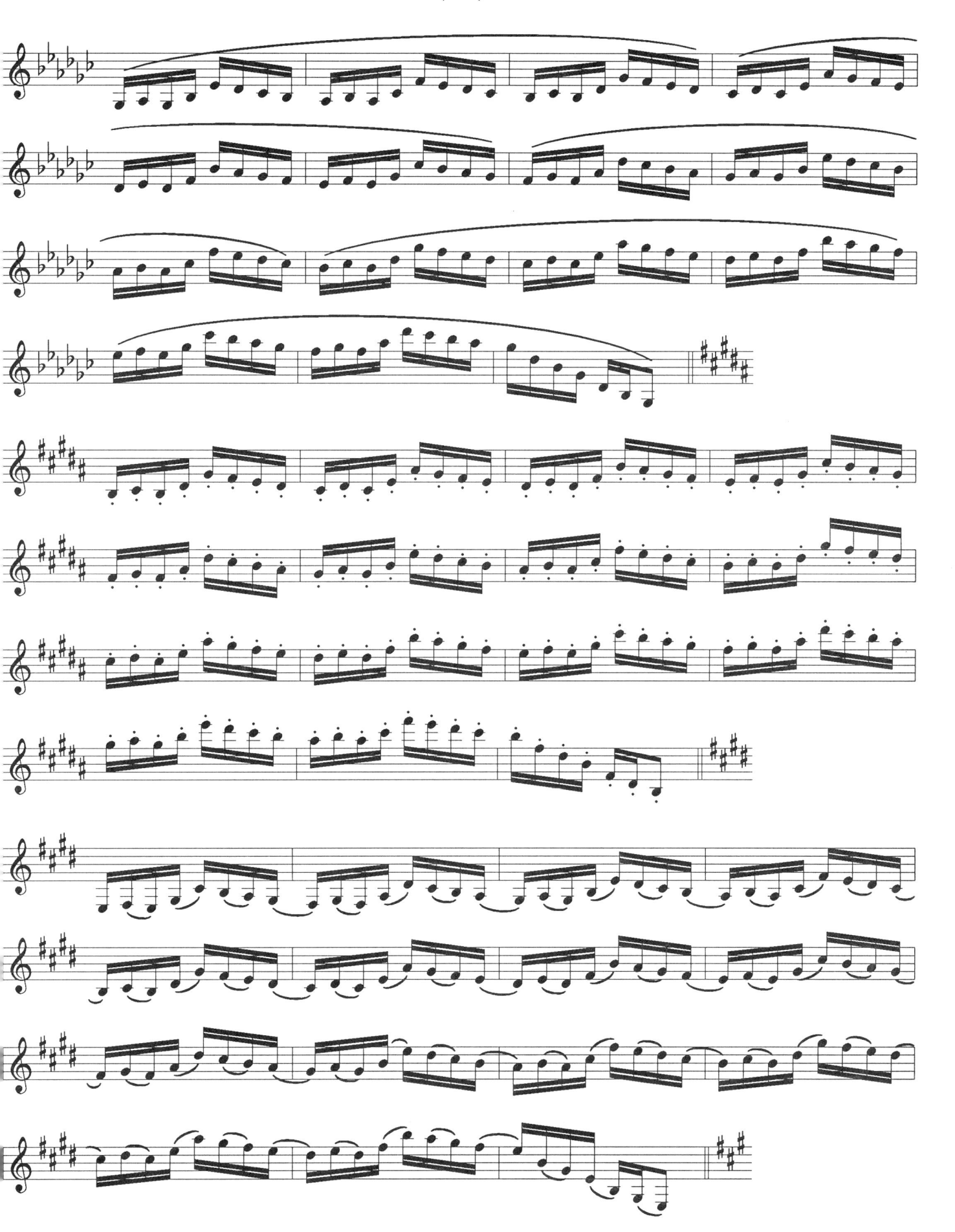

(Ex. 4)

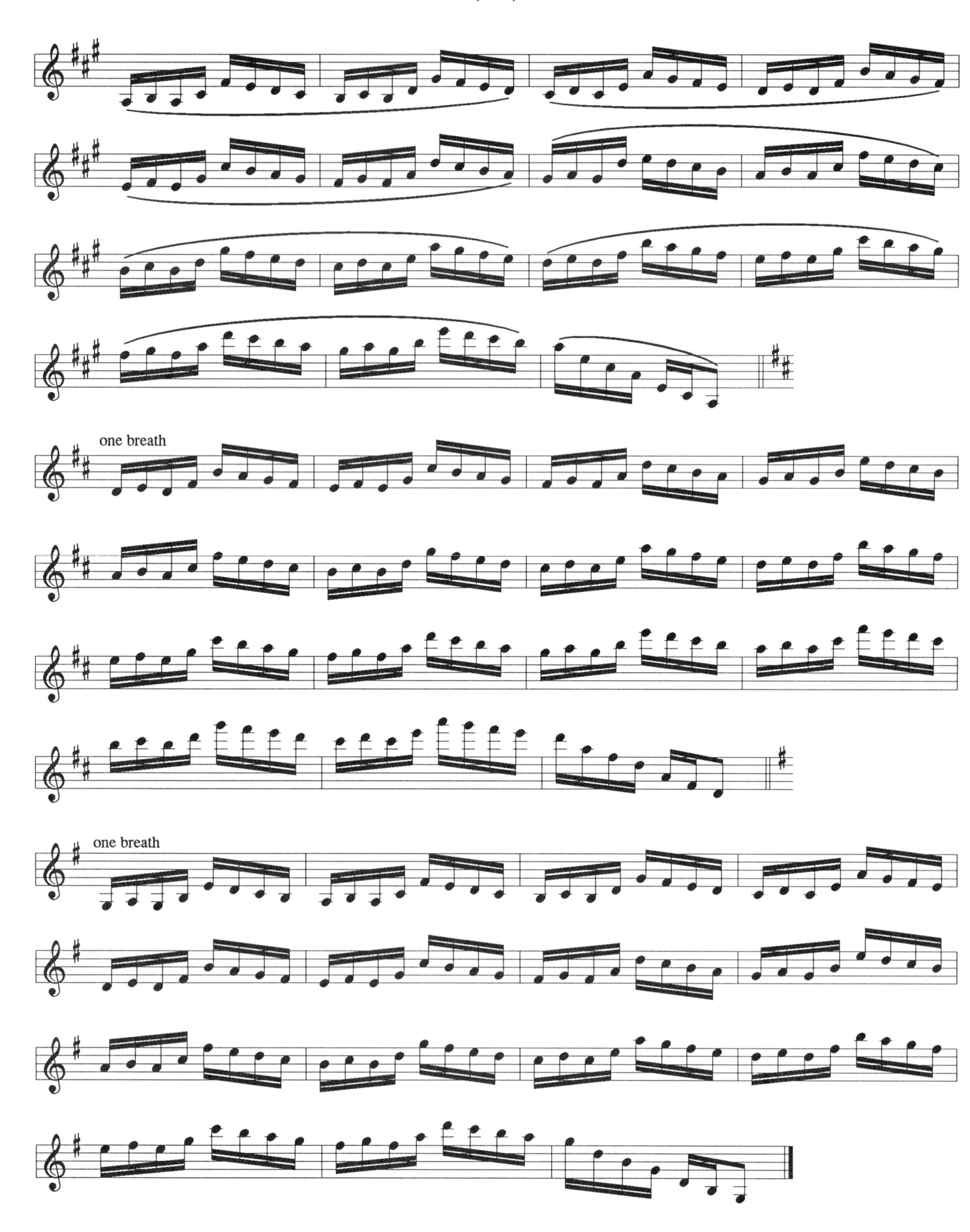

Ex. 5

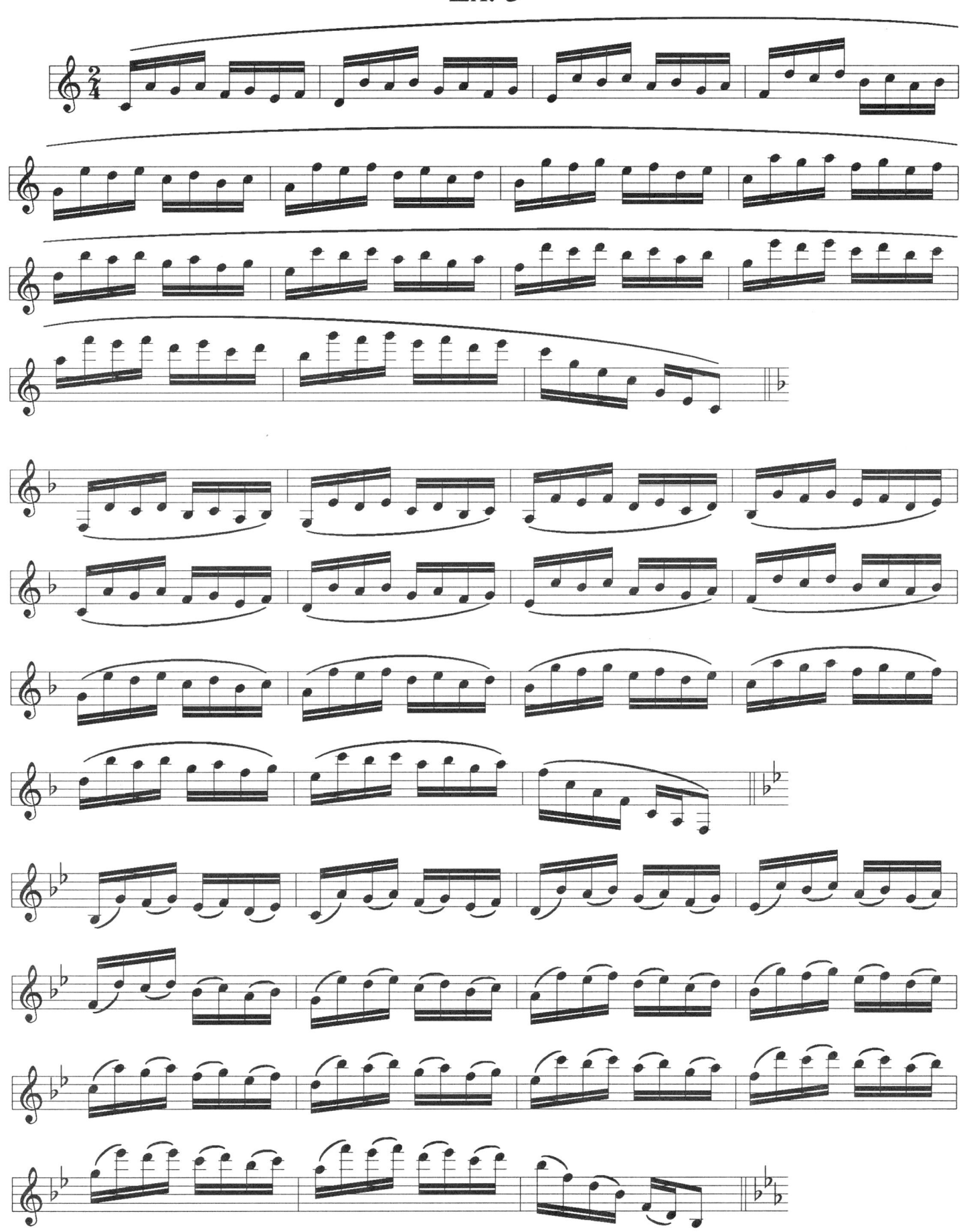

(Ex. 5)

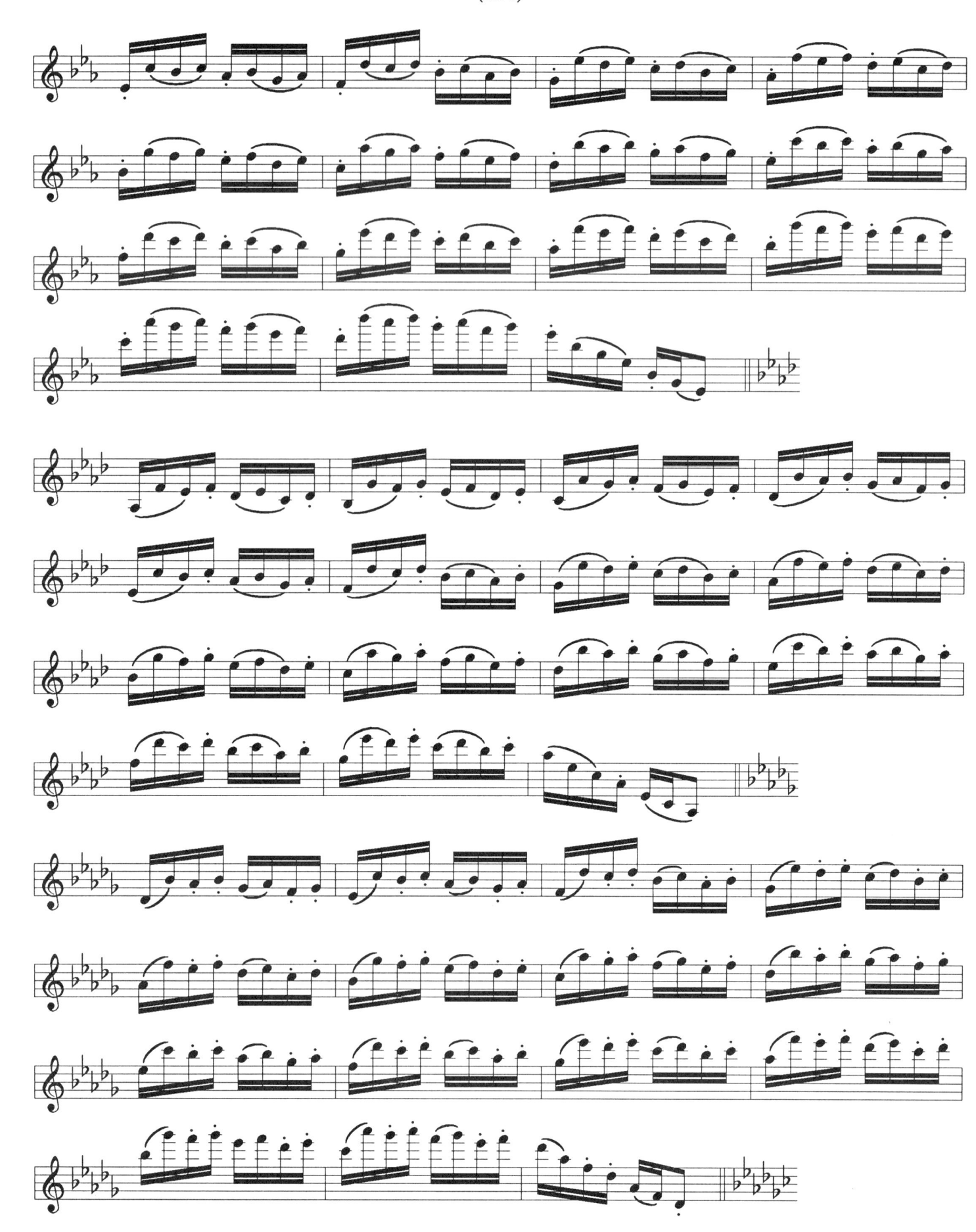

(Ex. 5)

(Ex. 5)

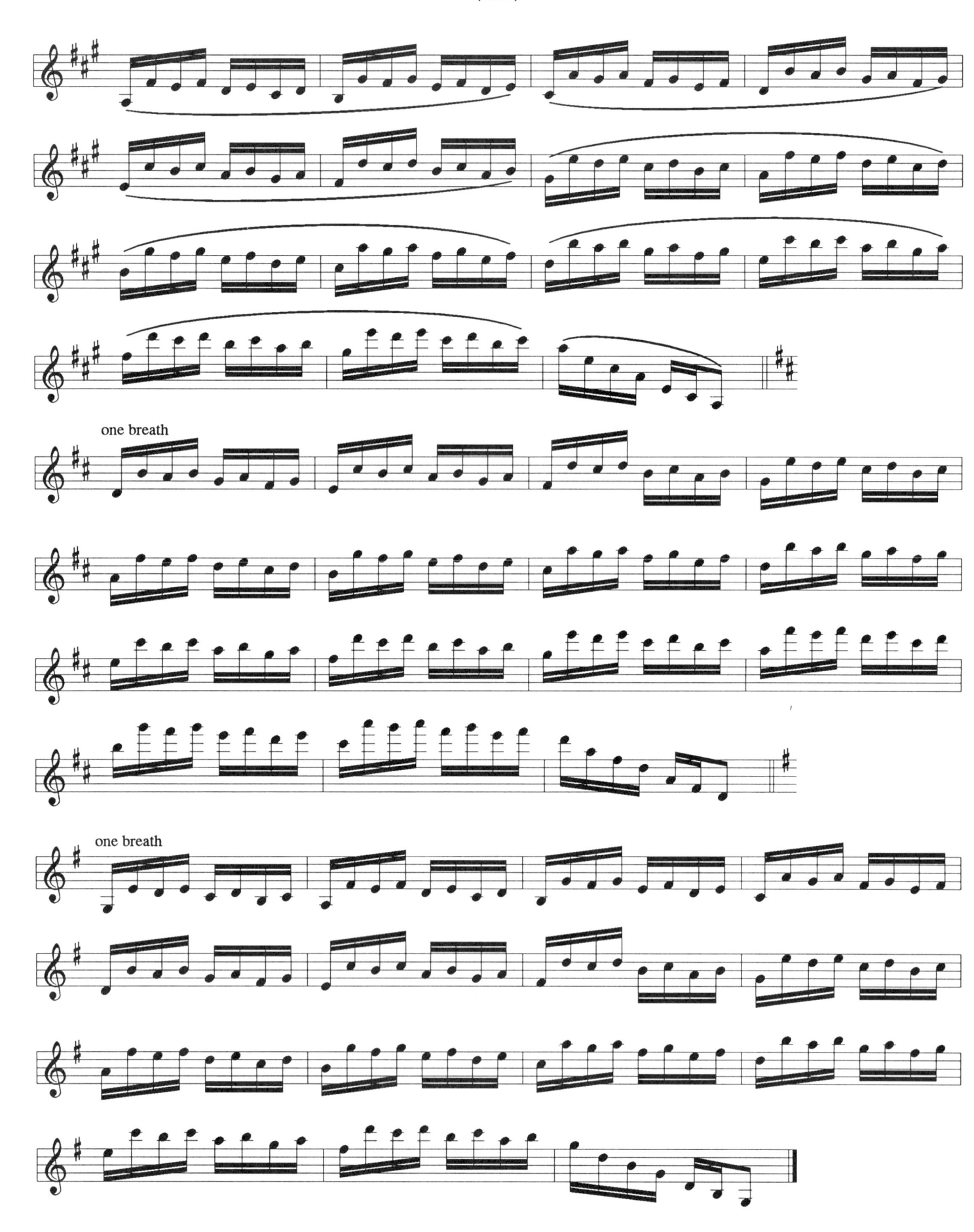

Ex. 6

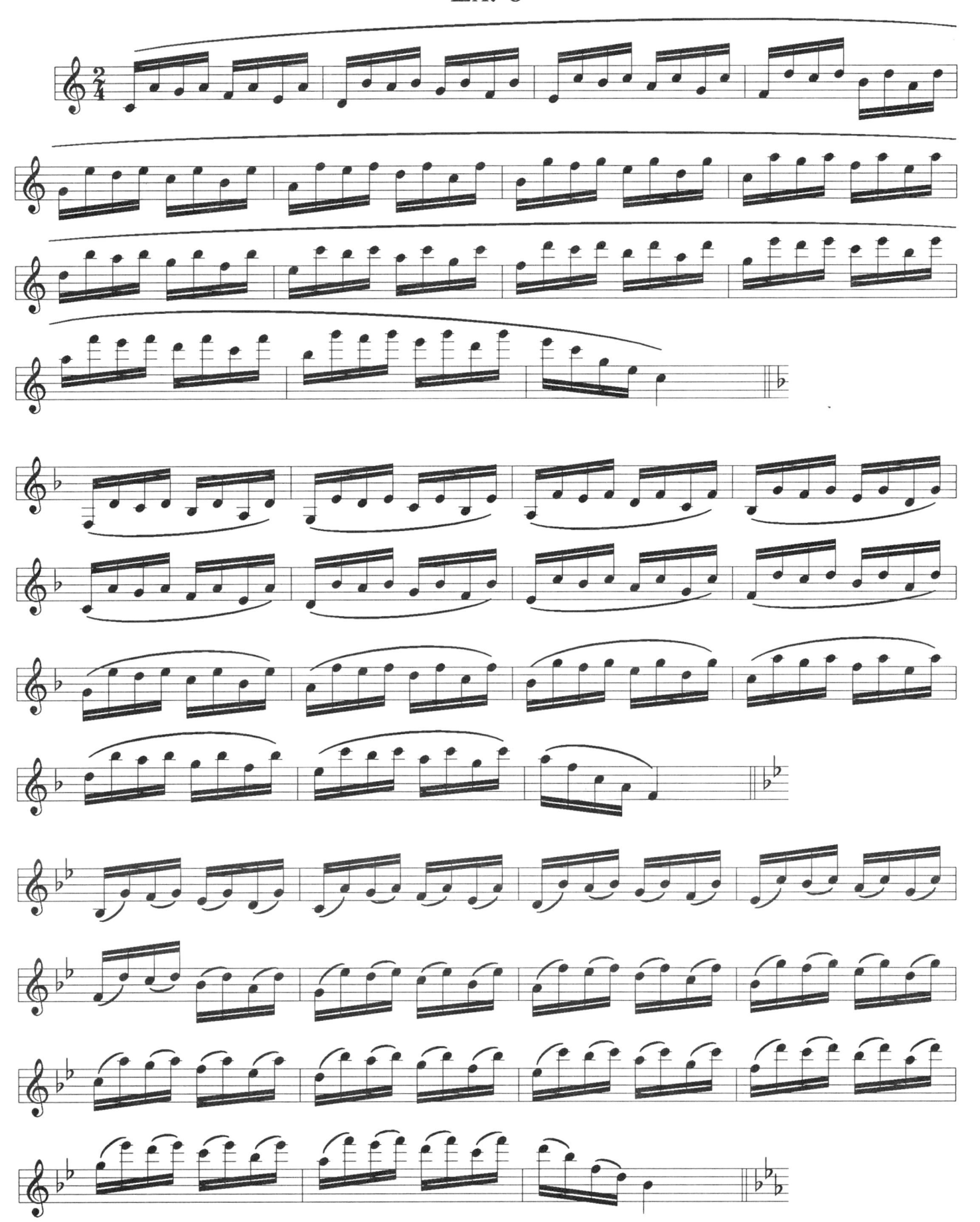

(Ex. 6)

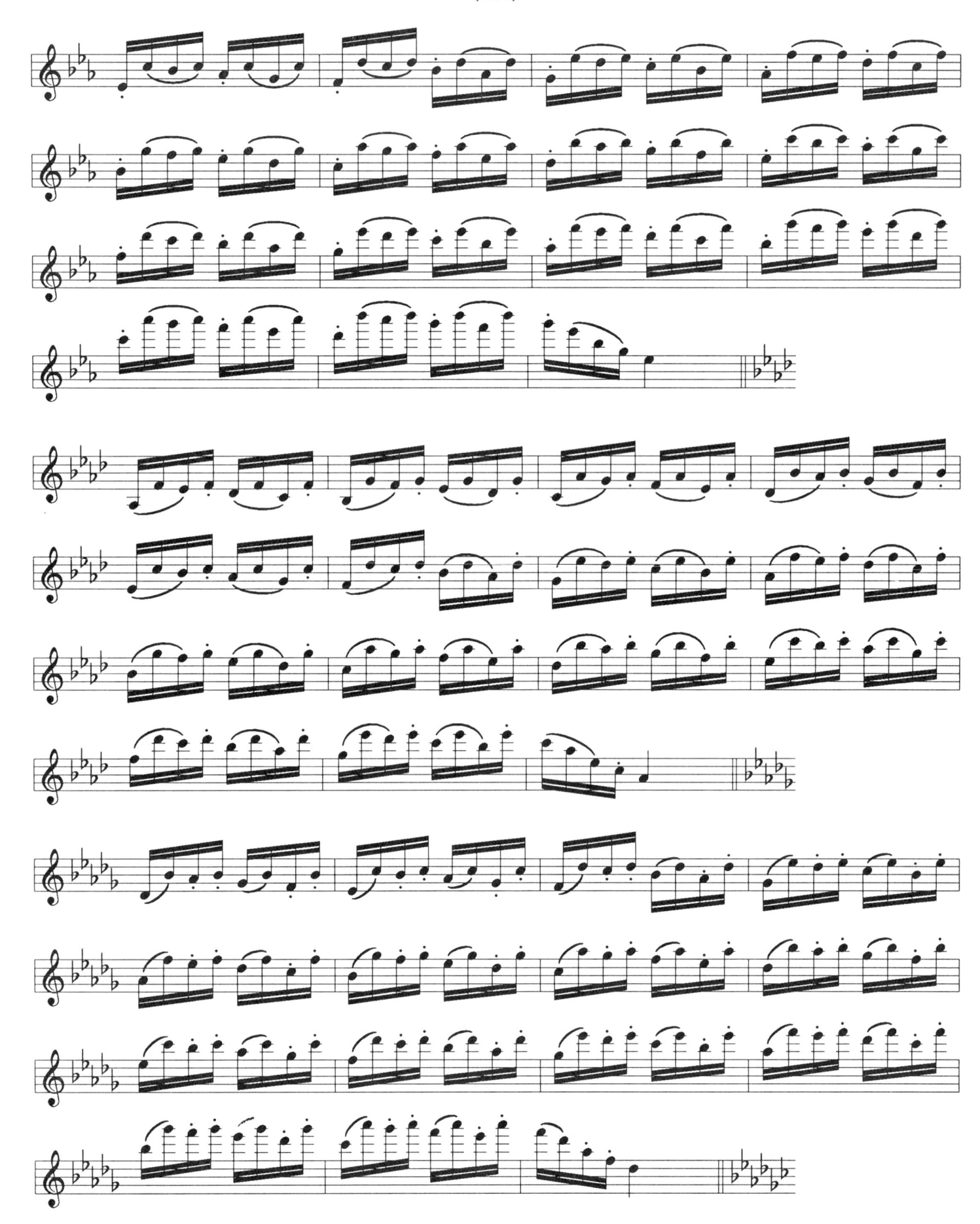

(Ex. 6)

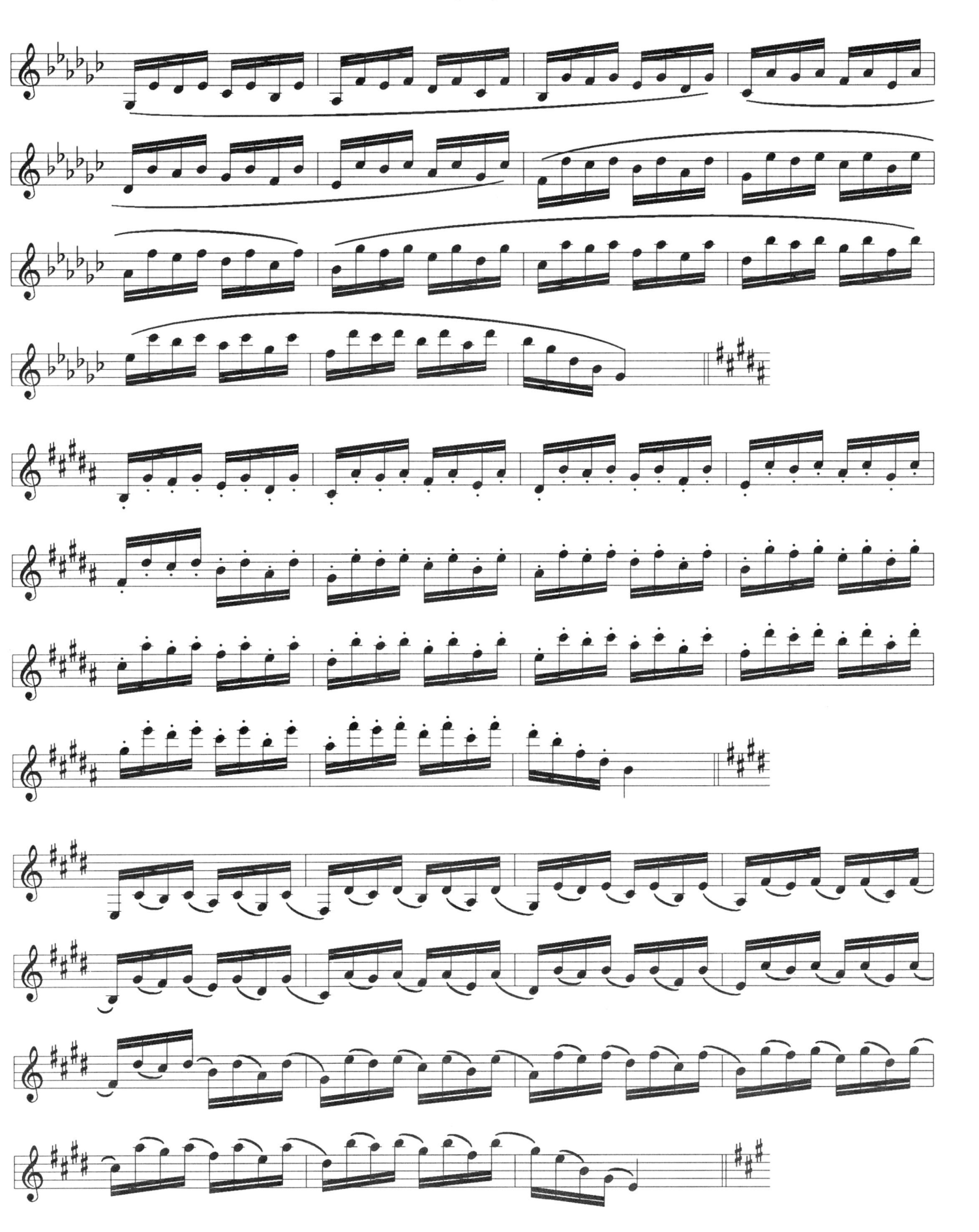

(Ex. 6)

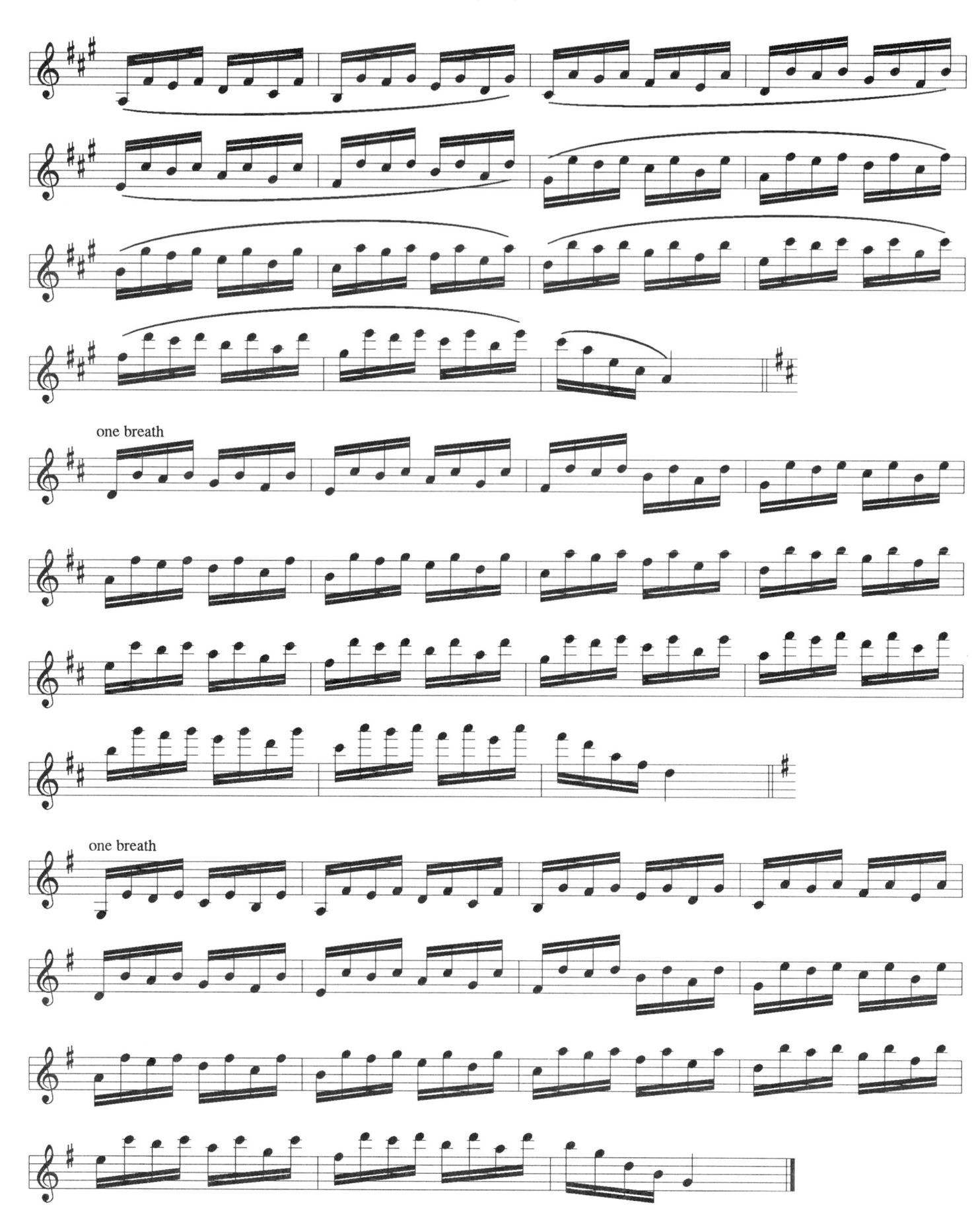

Ex. 7

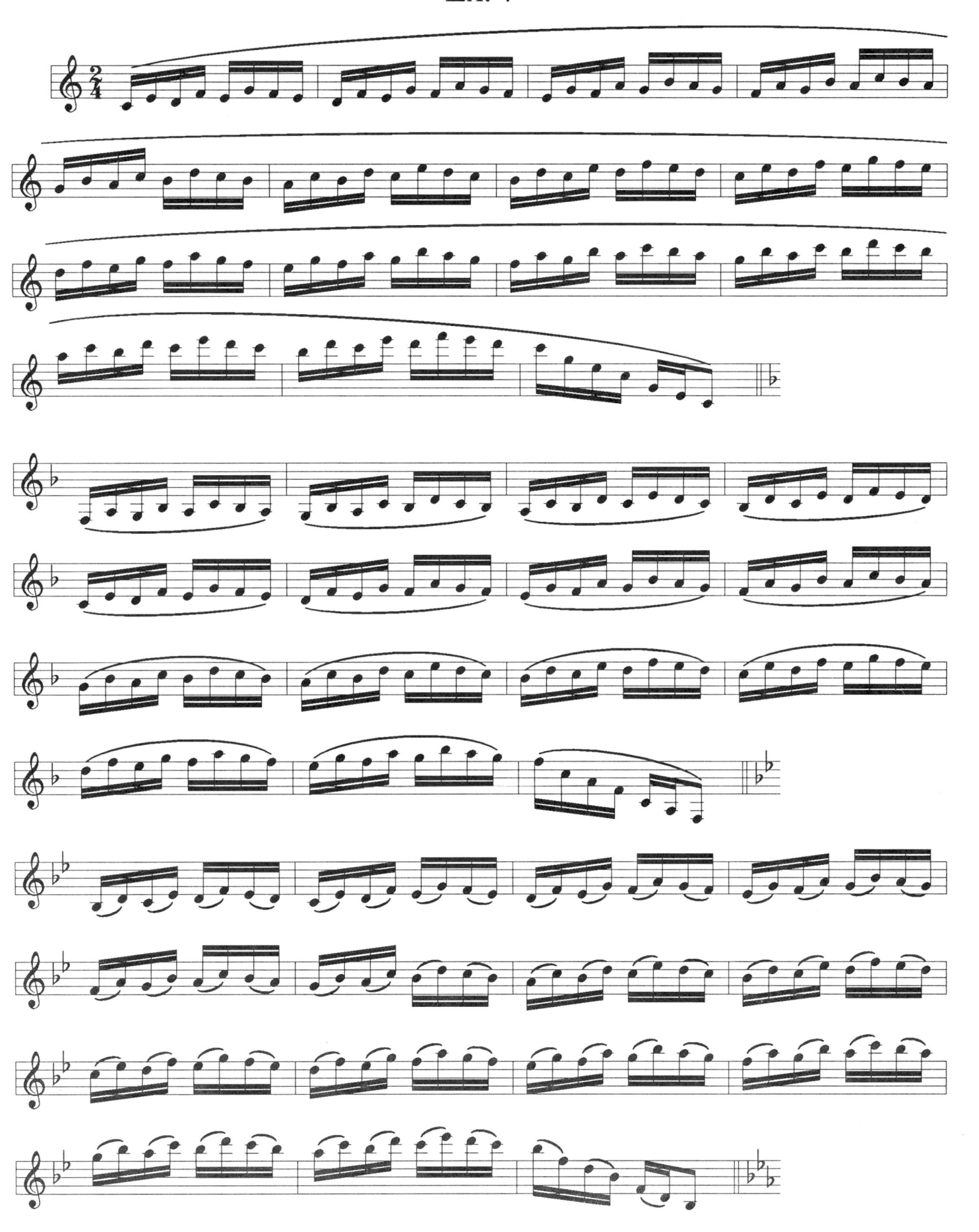

(Ex. 7)

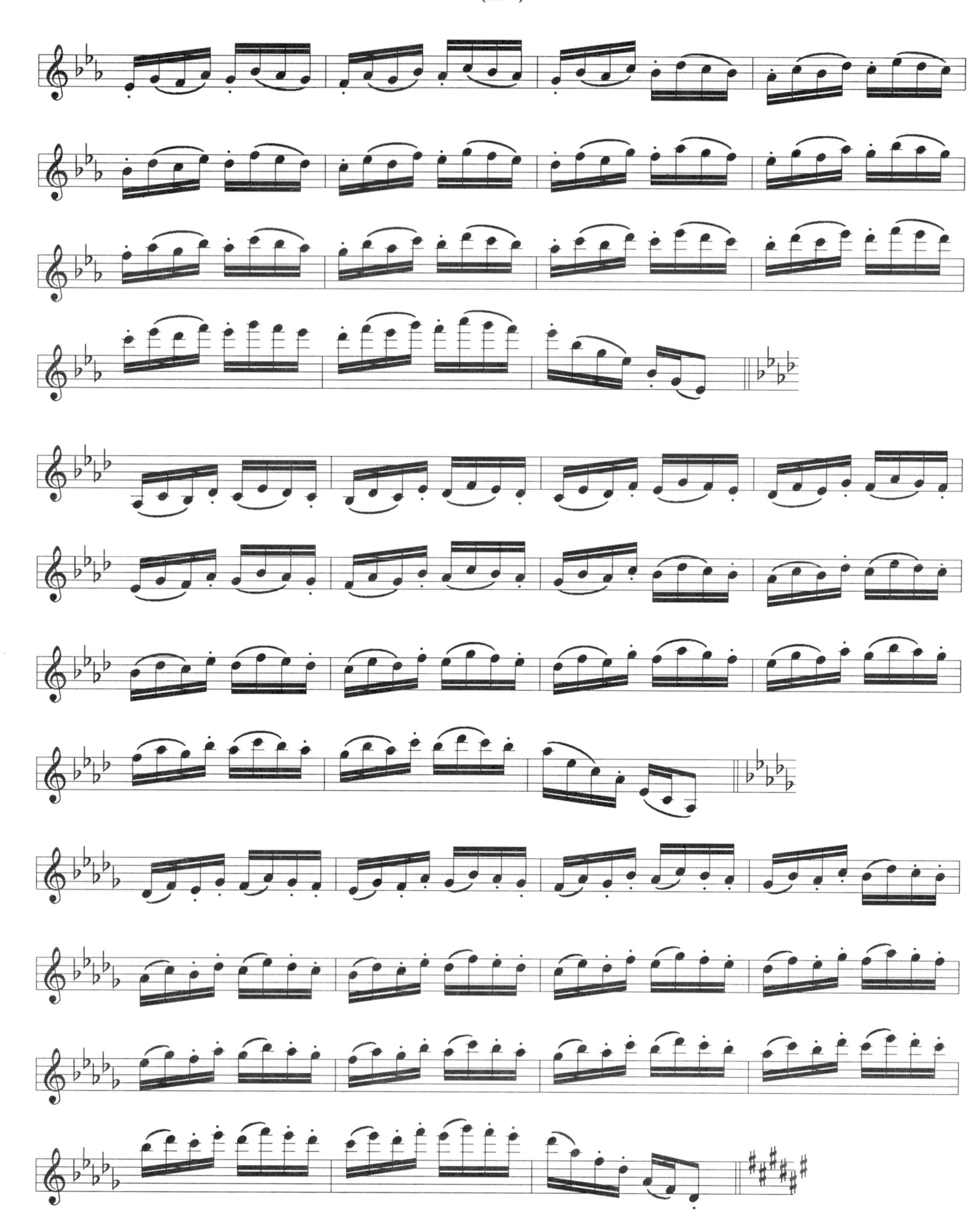

(Ex. 7)

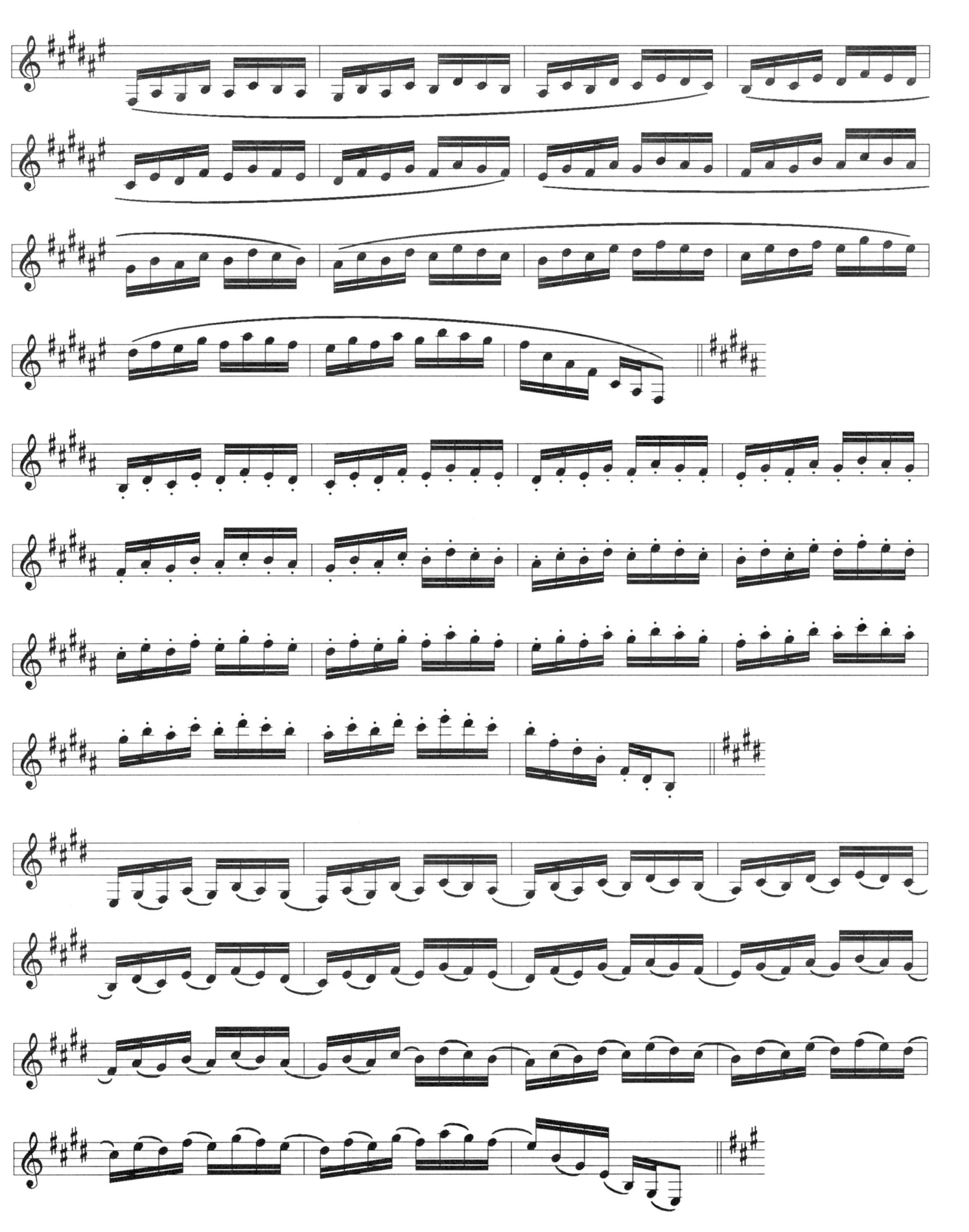

(Ex. 7)

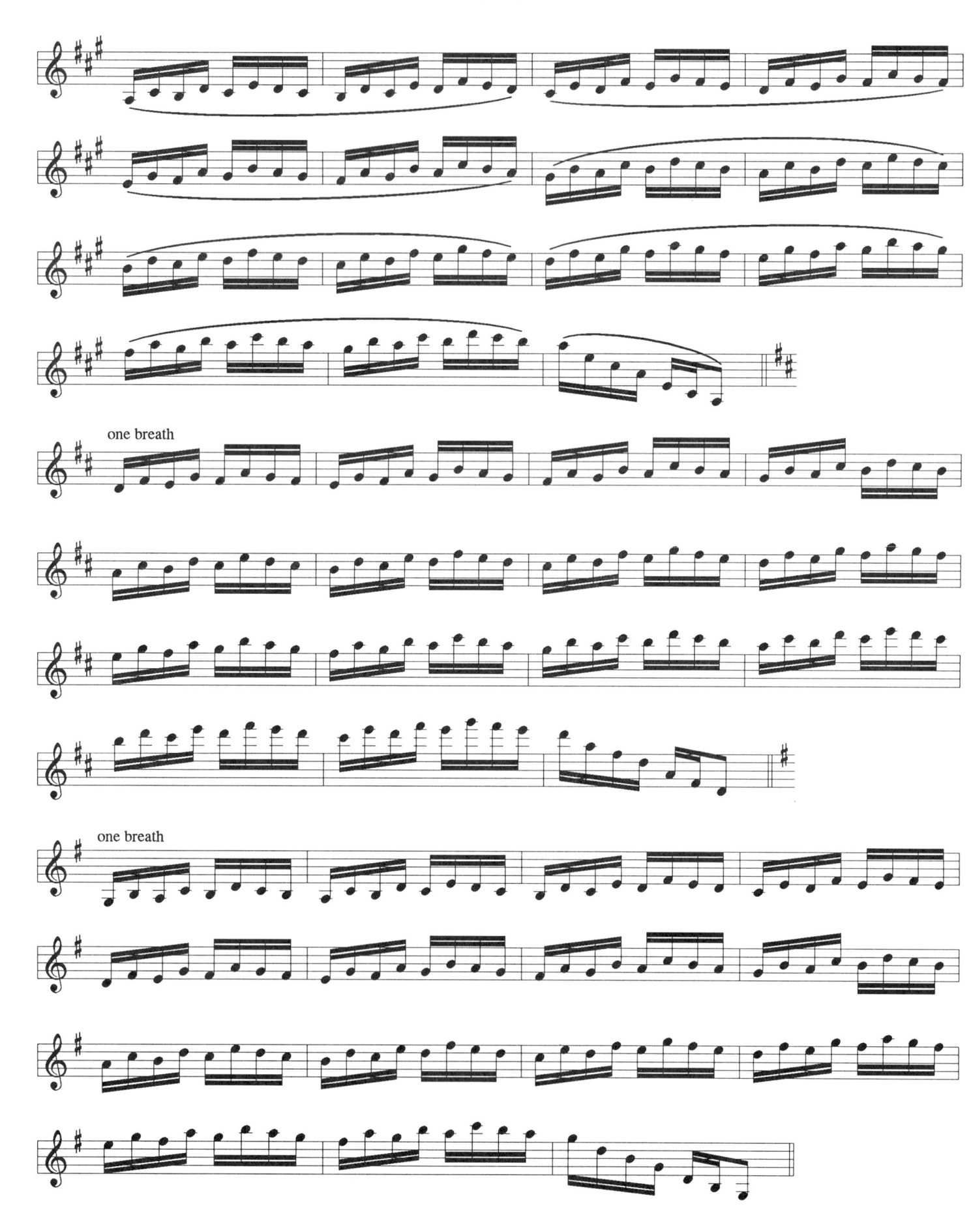

Ex. 8

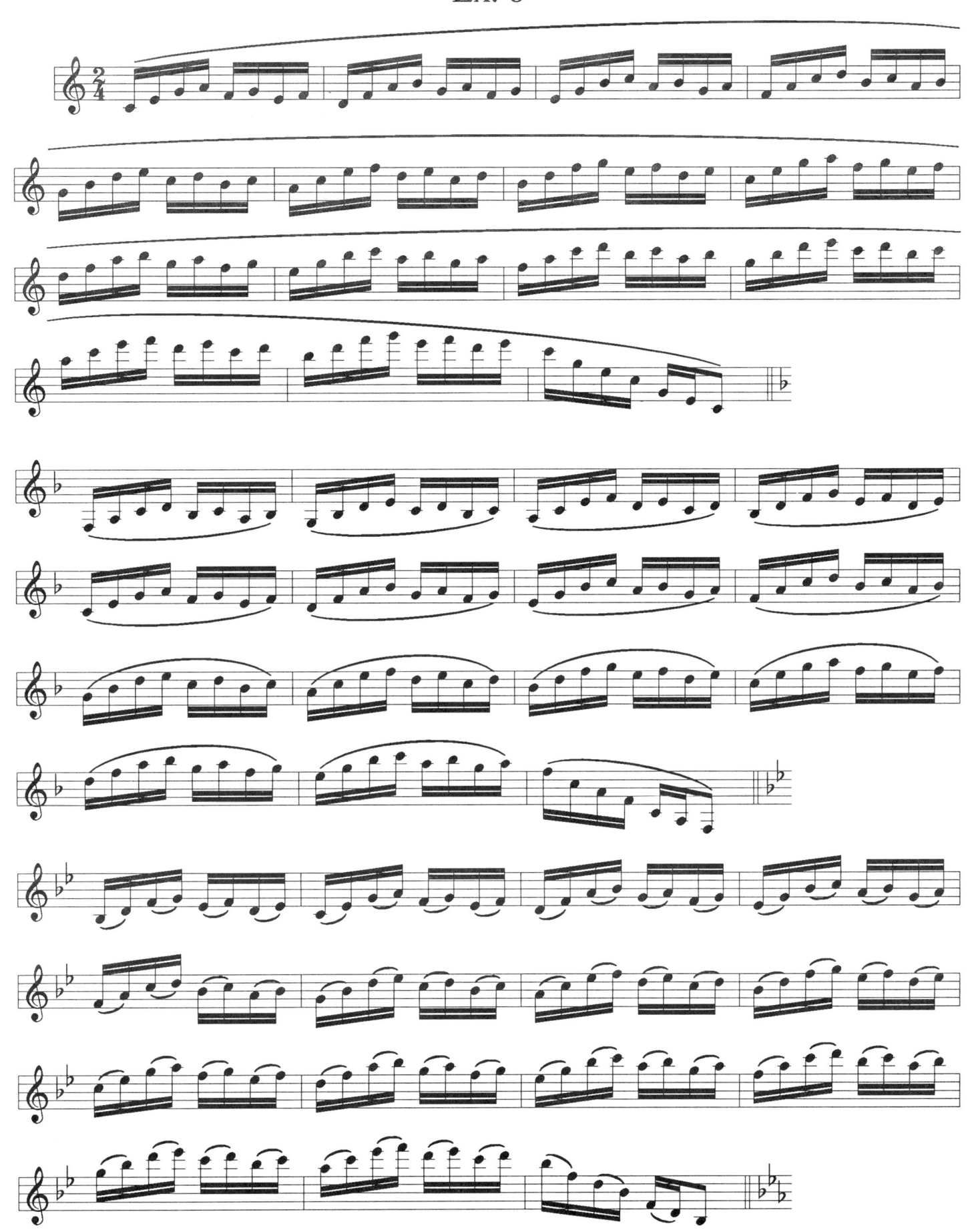

(Ex. 8)

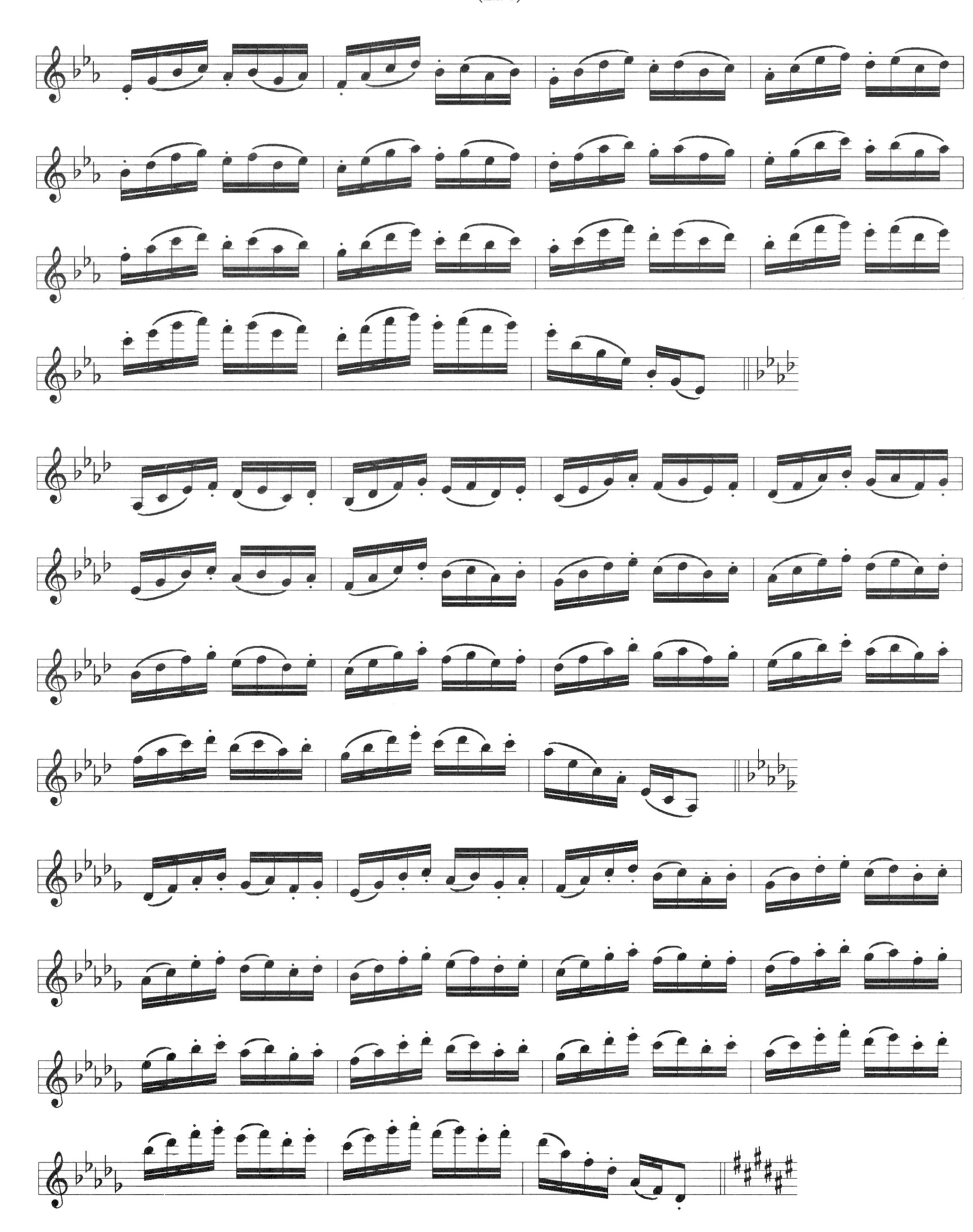

(Ex. 8)

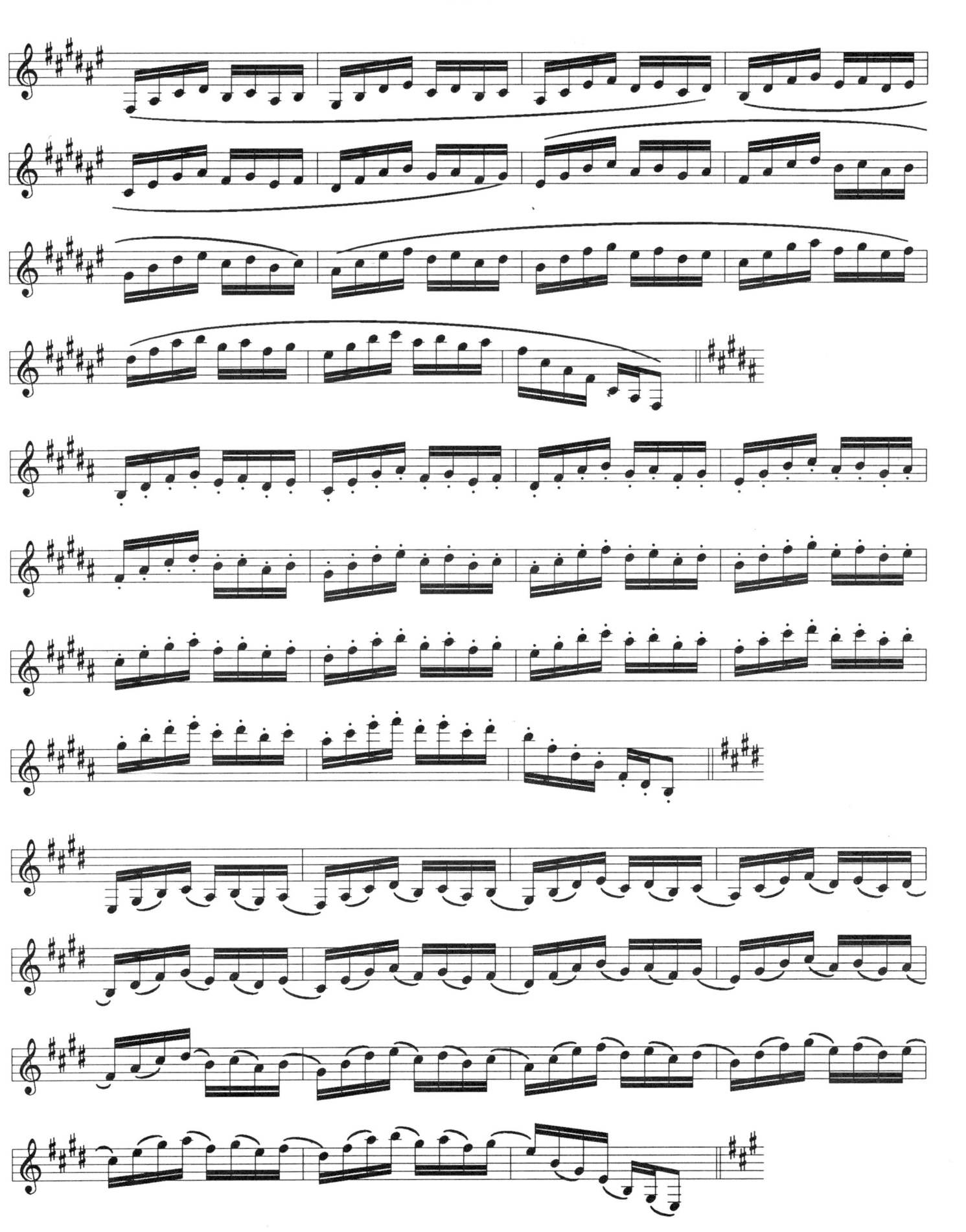

(Ex. 8)

Ex. 9

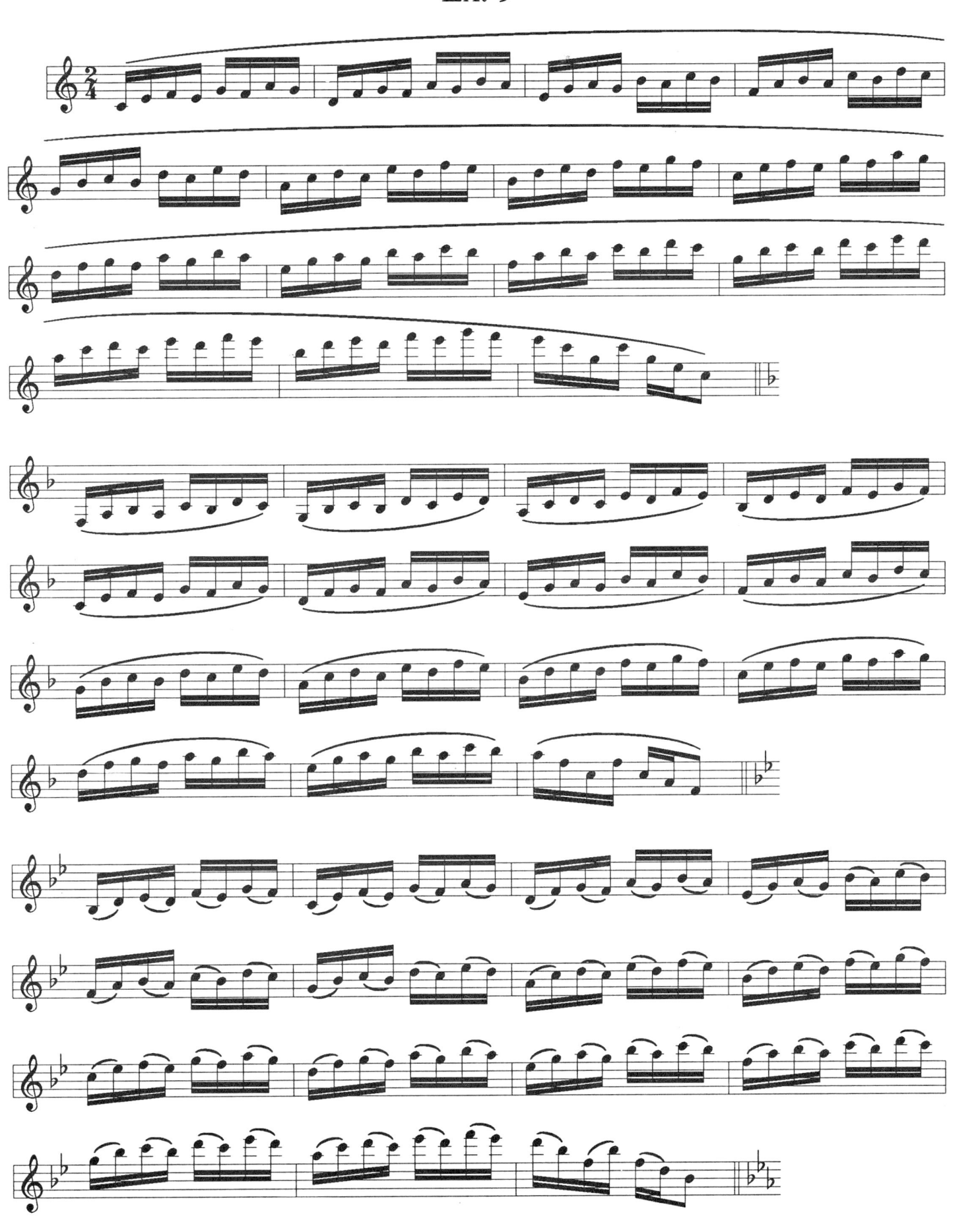

(Ex. 9)

(Ex. 9)

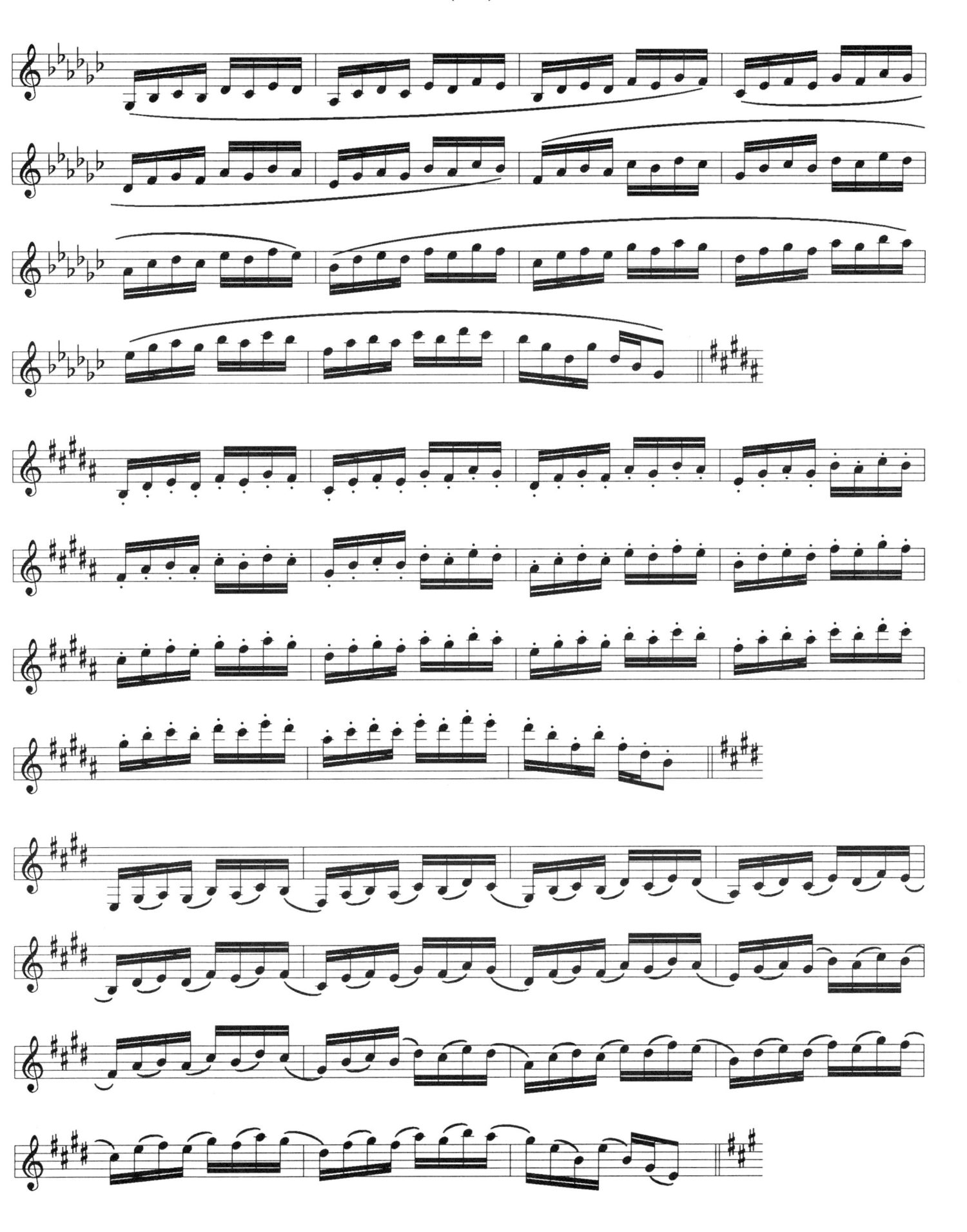

(Ex. 9)

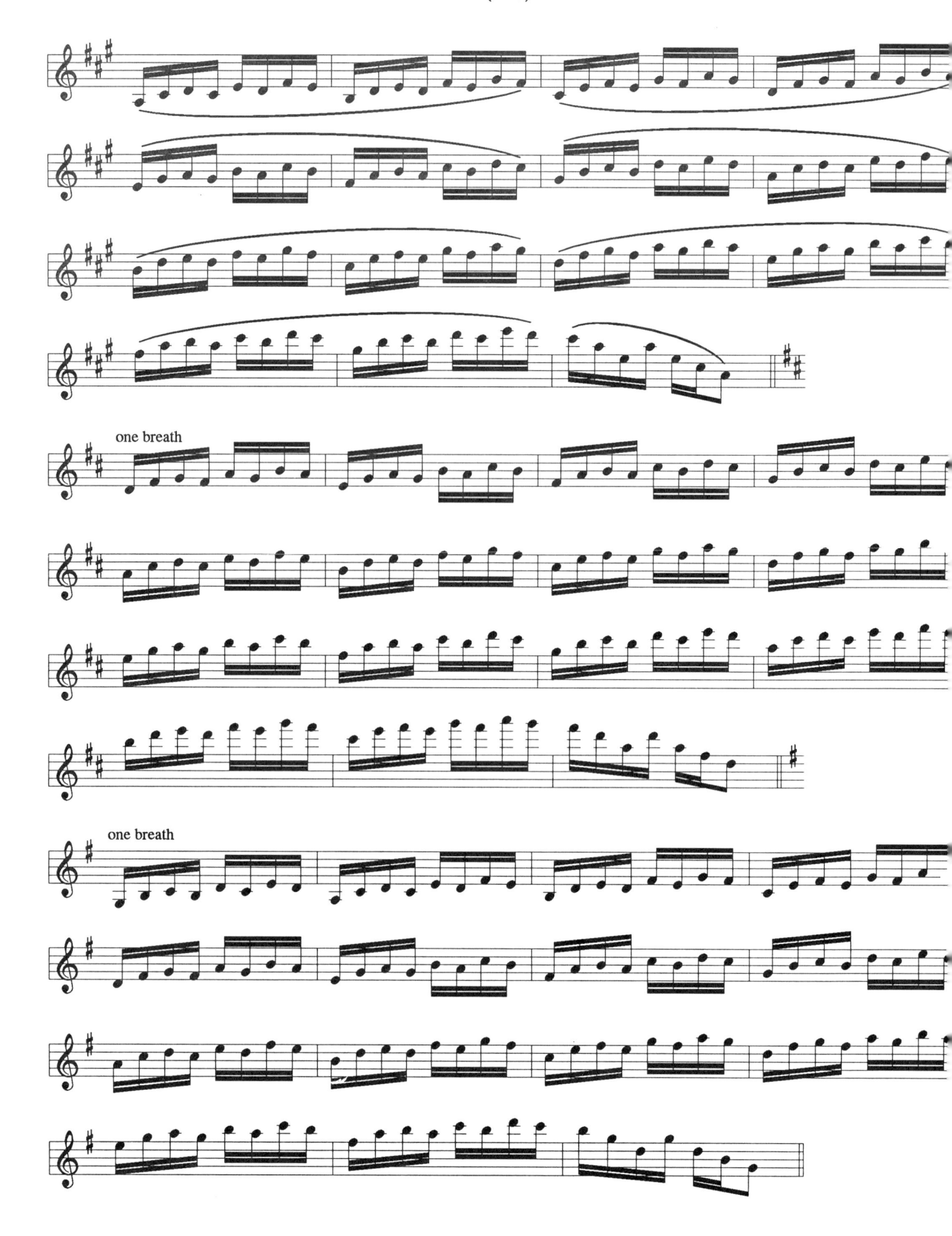

Ex. 10

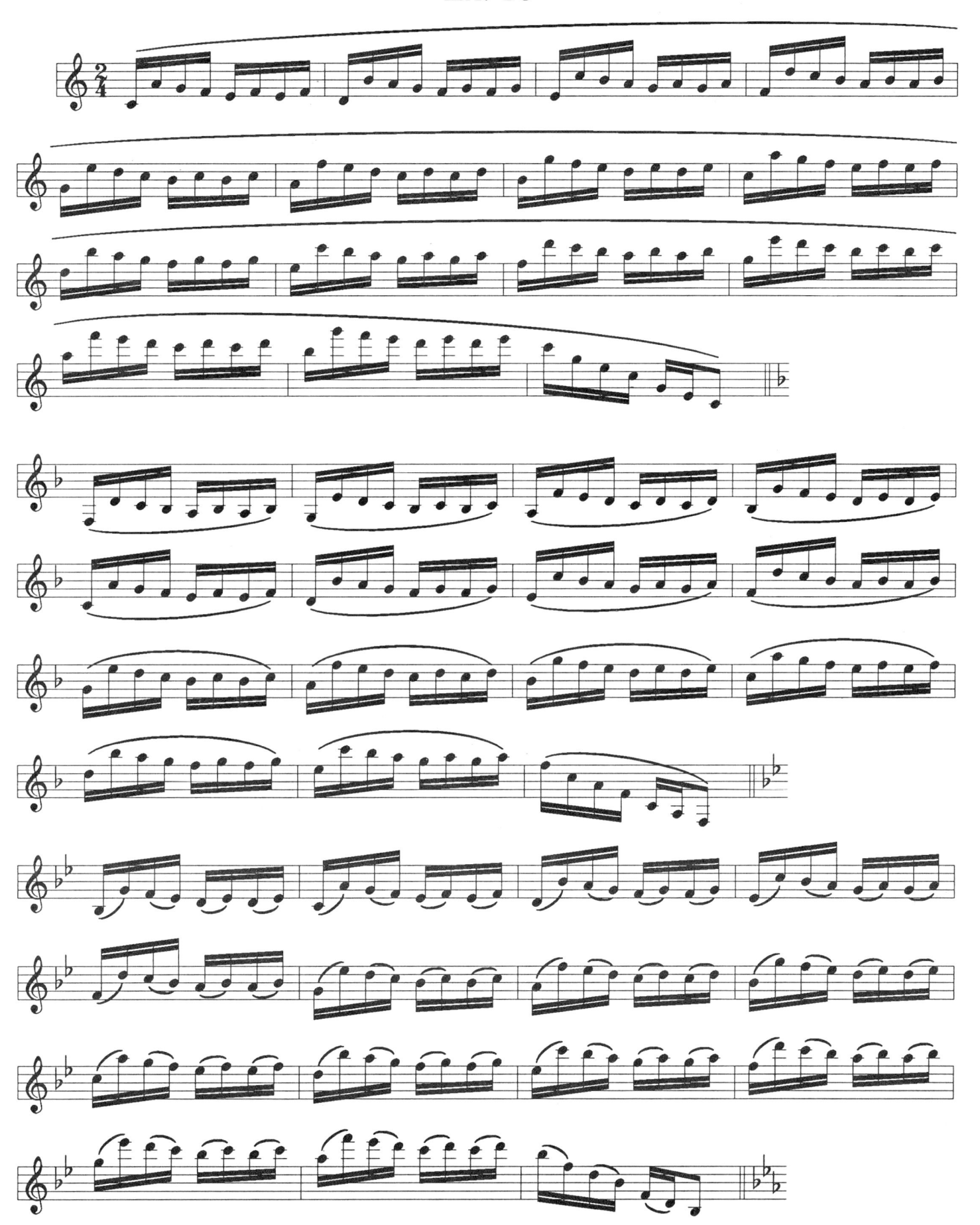

(Ex. 10)

(Ex. 10)

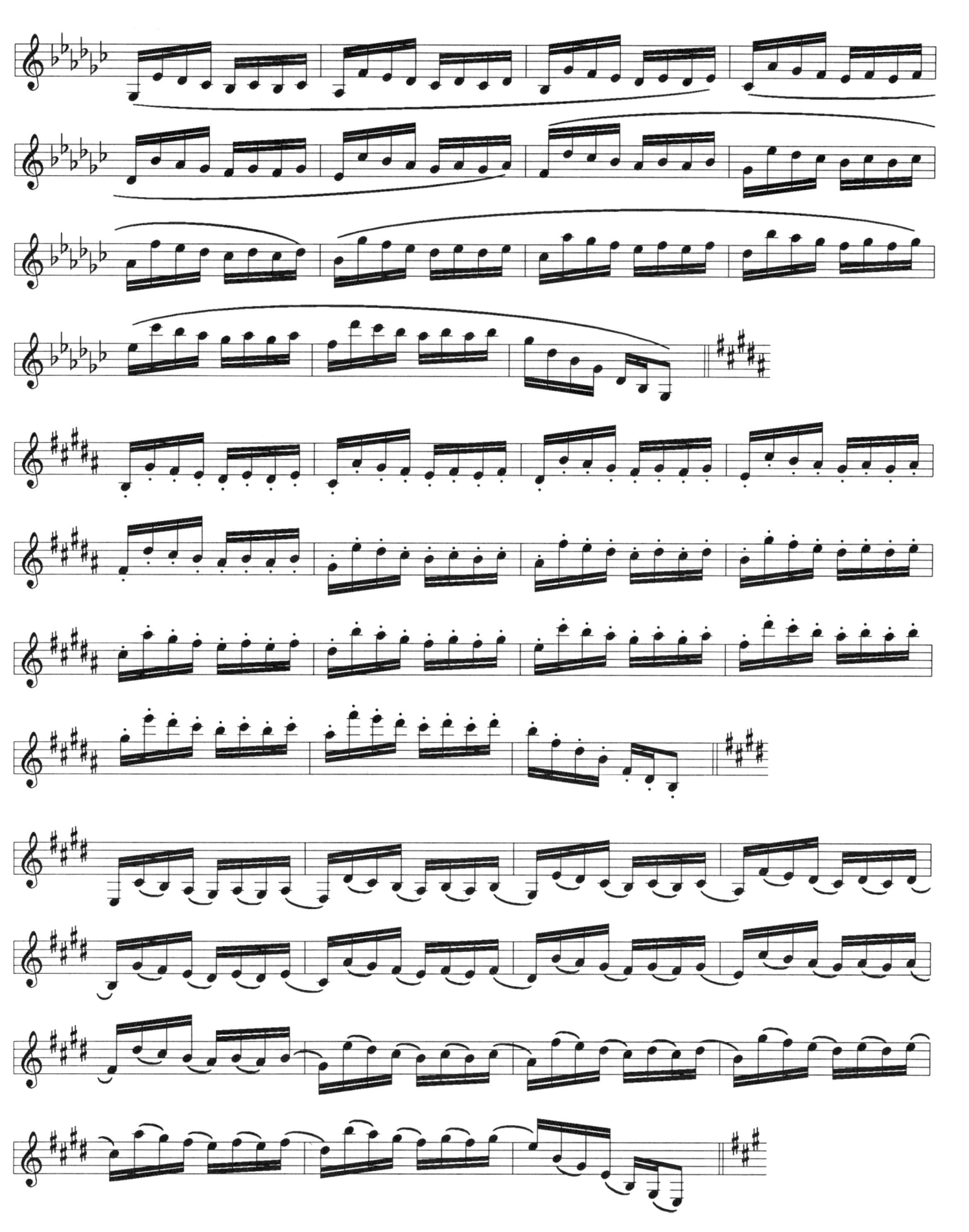

(Ex. 10)

Ex. 11

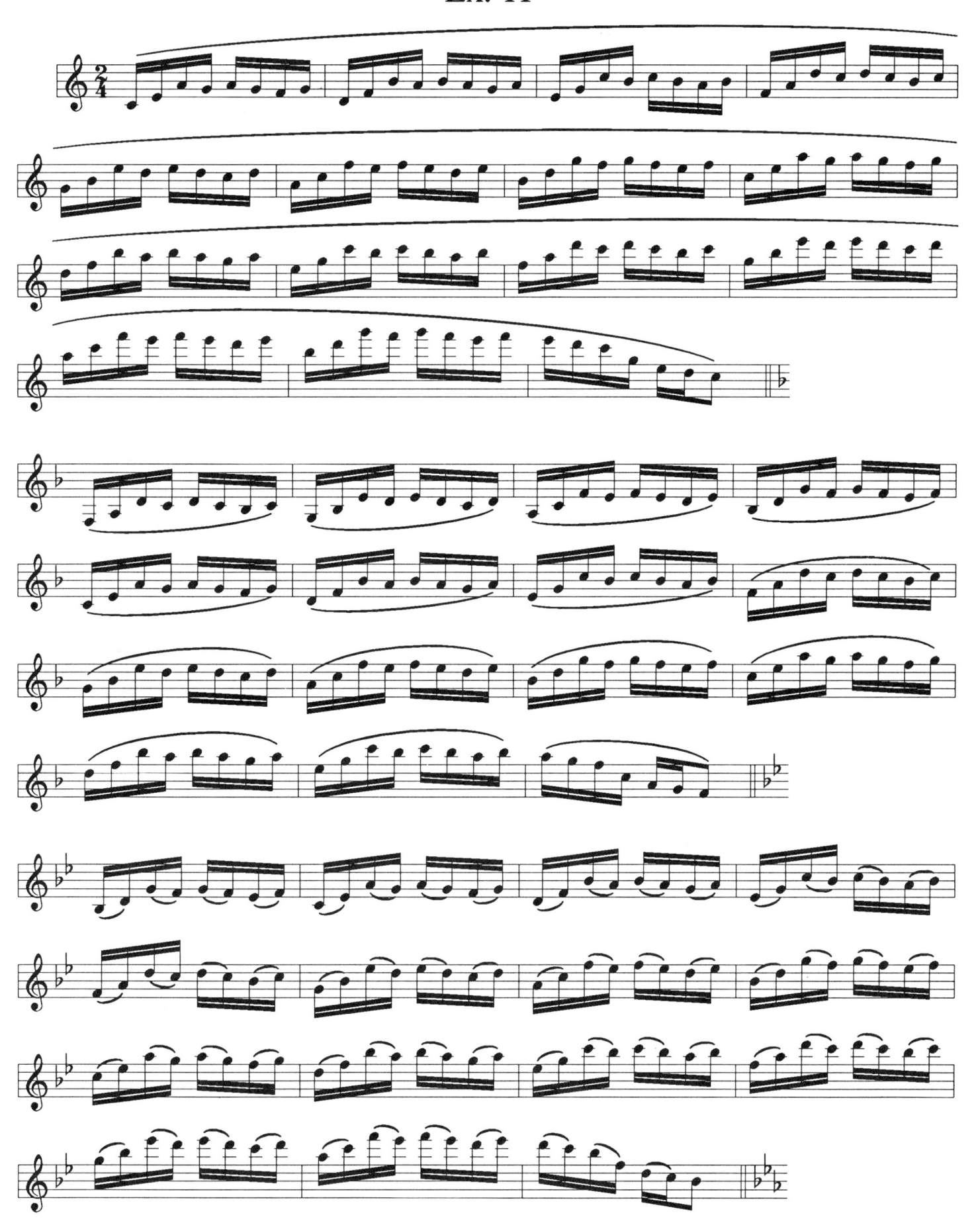

(Ex. 11)

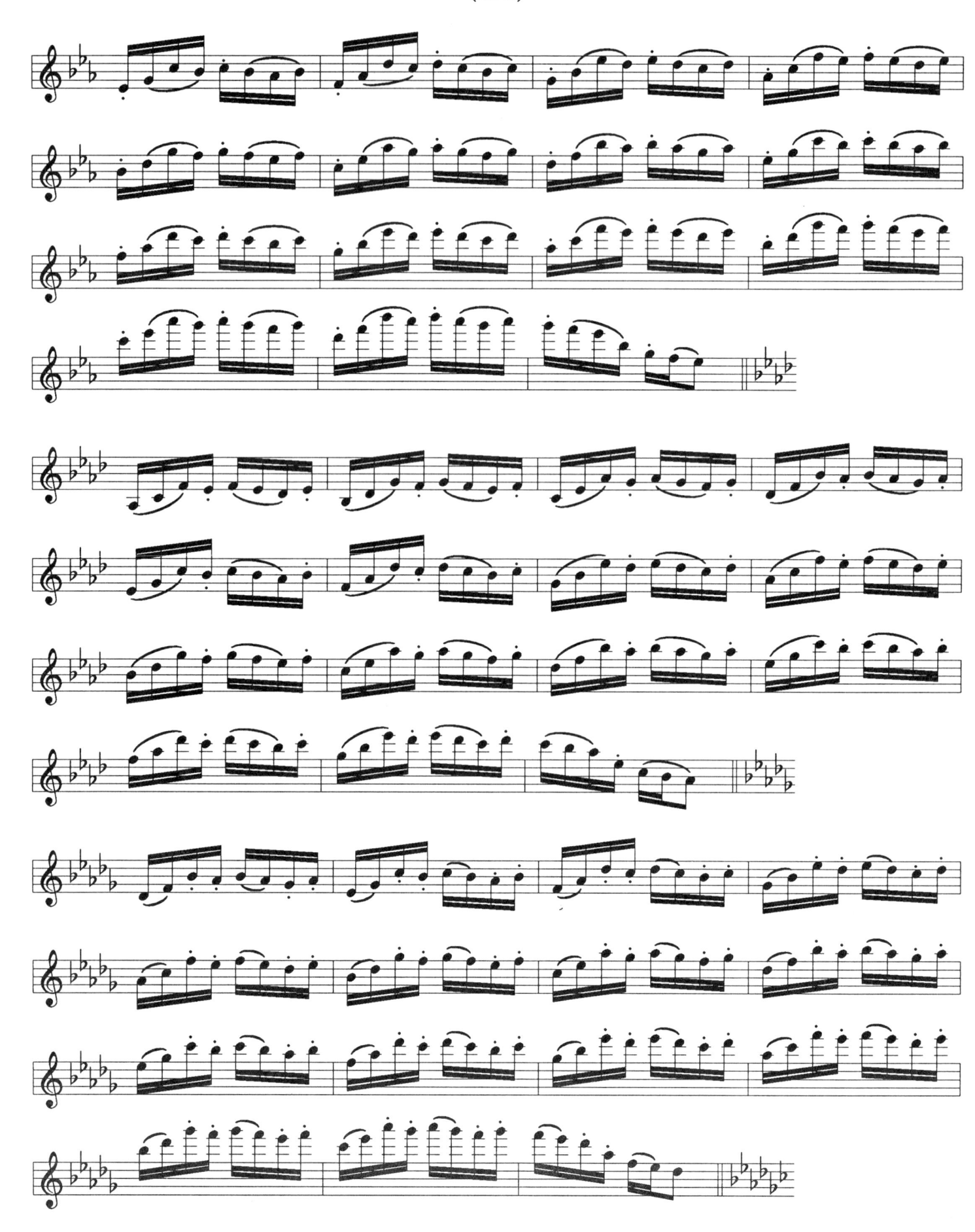

(Ex. 11)

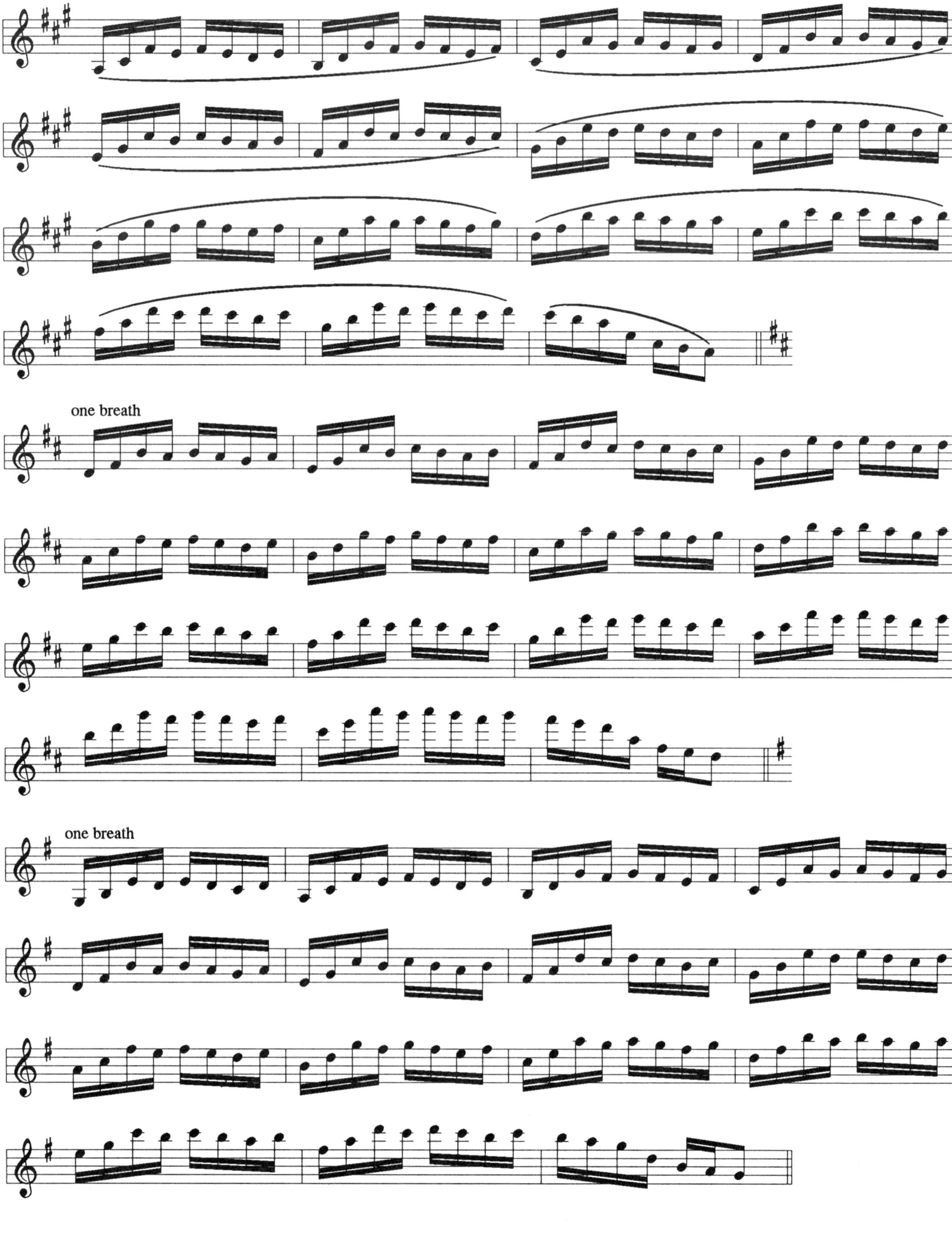
one breath
one breath

Ex. 12

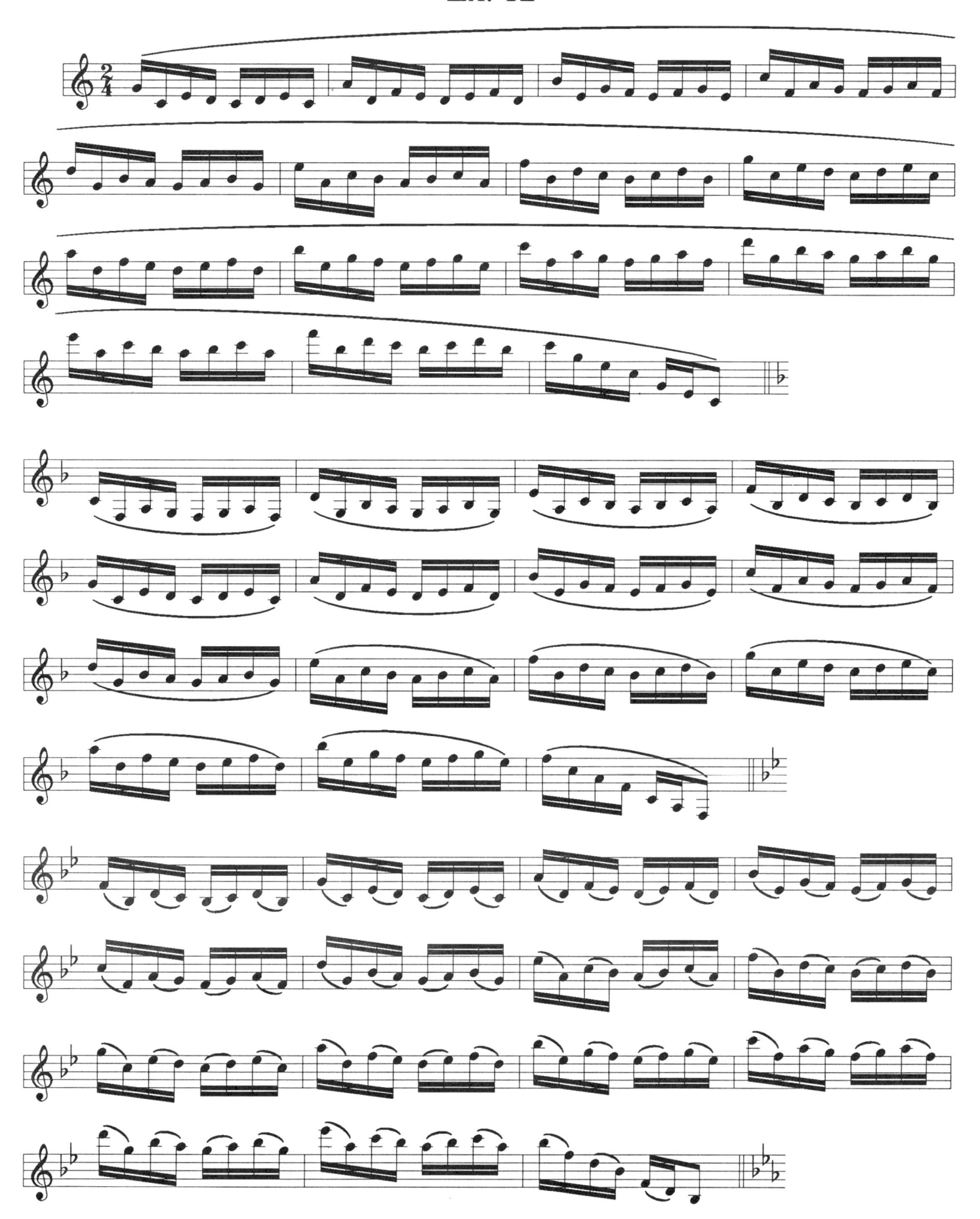

(Ex. 12)

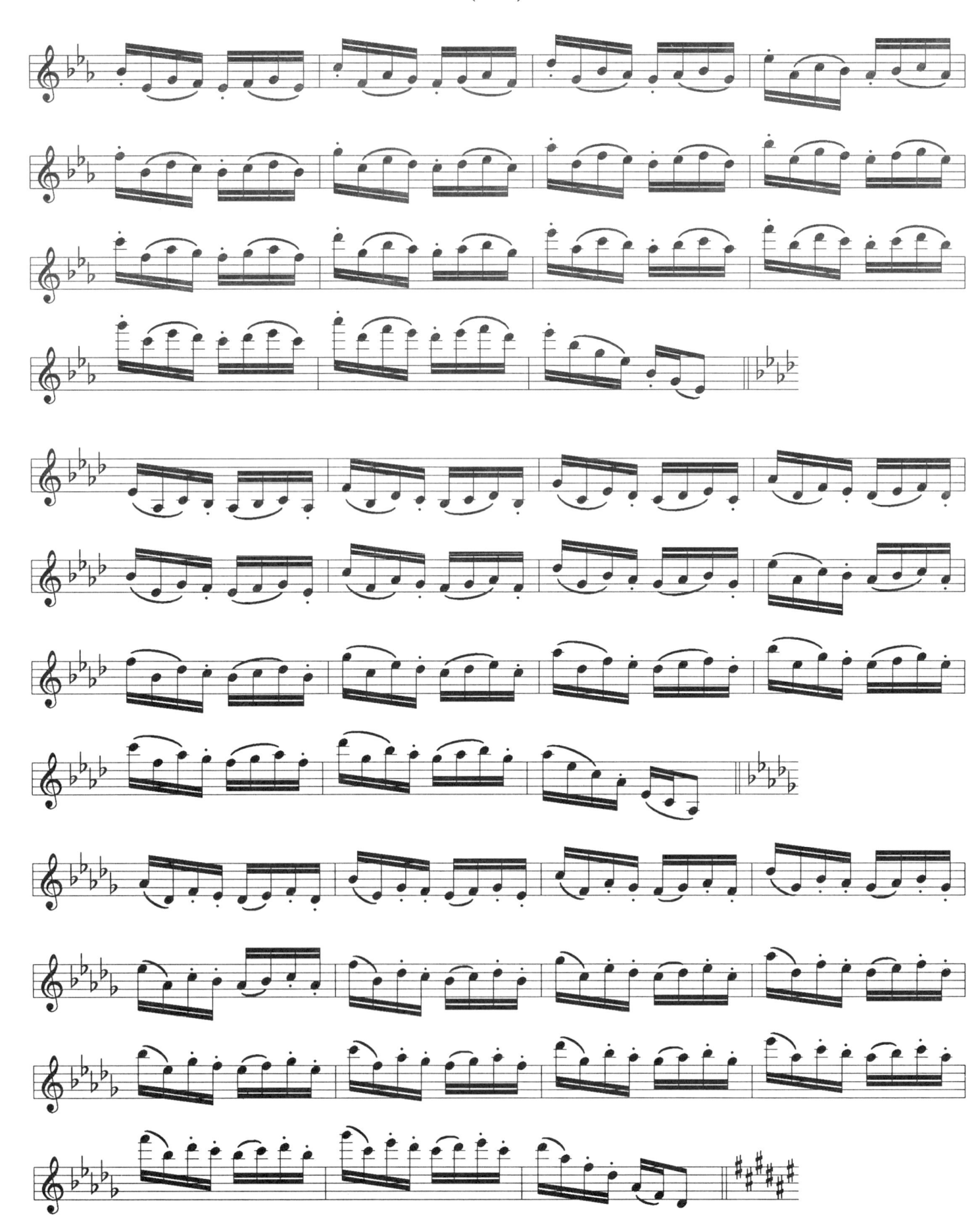

(Ex. 12)

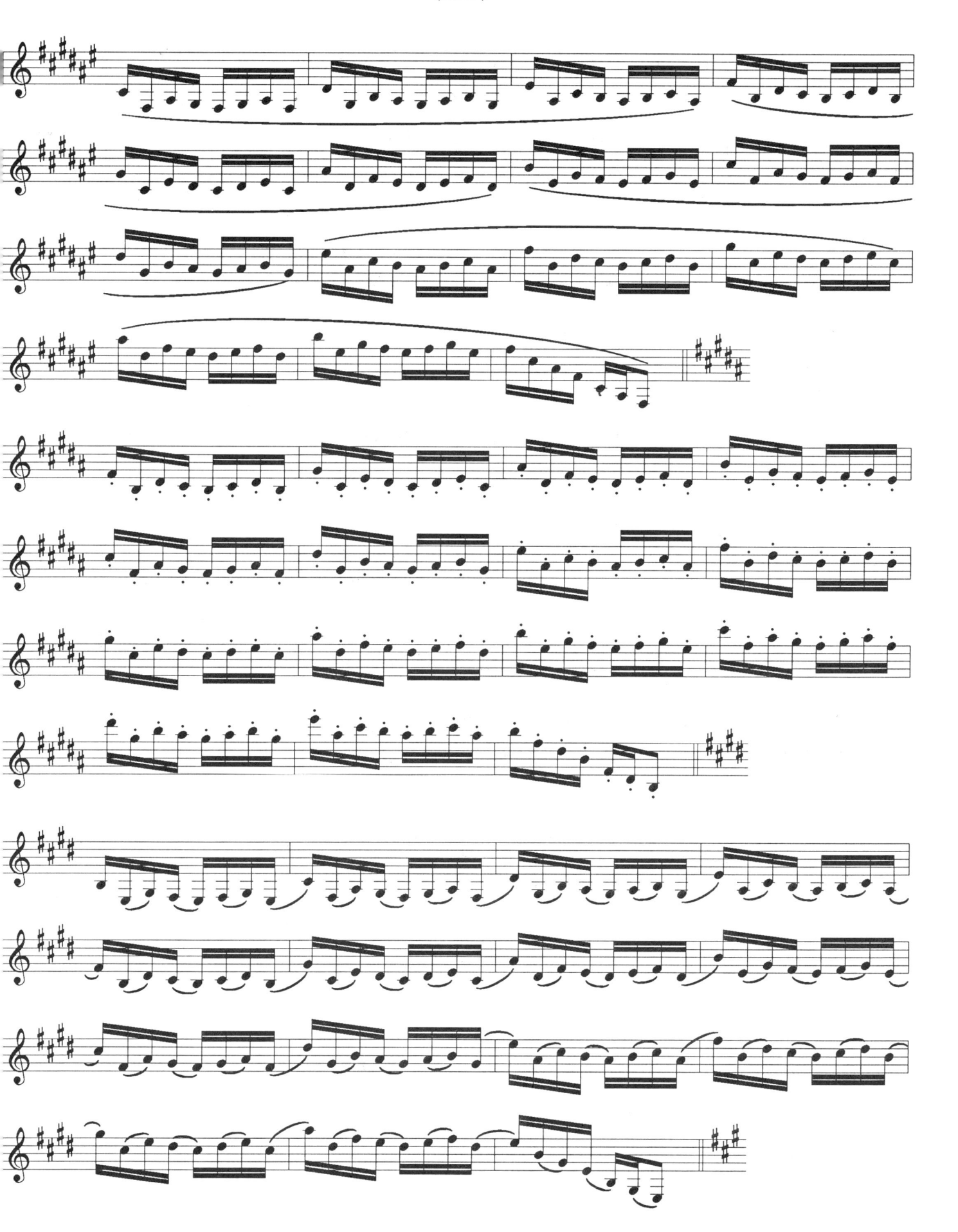

(Ex. 12)

Try to play each exercise with one breath.

Exercise 13

Ex. 13   pg. 2

Ex. 13 pg. 3

Ex. 13 pg. 4

Ex. 13   pg. 5

Exercise 14

Try to play each exercise with one breath

Ex. 14   pg. 2

Ex. 14 pg. 3

Ex. 14   pg. 4

Ex. 14   pg. 5

Exercise 15

Try to play each exercise with one breath

Ex. 15   pg. 2

Ex. 15   pg. 3

Ex. 15 pg. 4

Ex. 15 pg. 5

Any articulation you desire

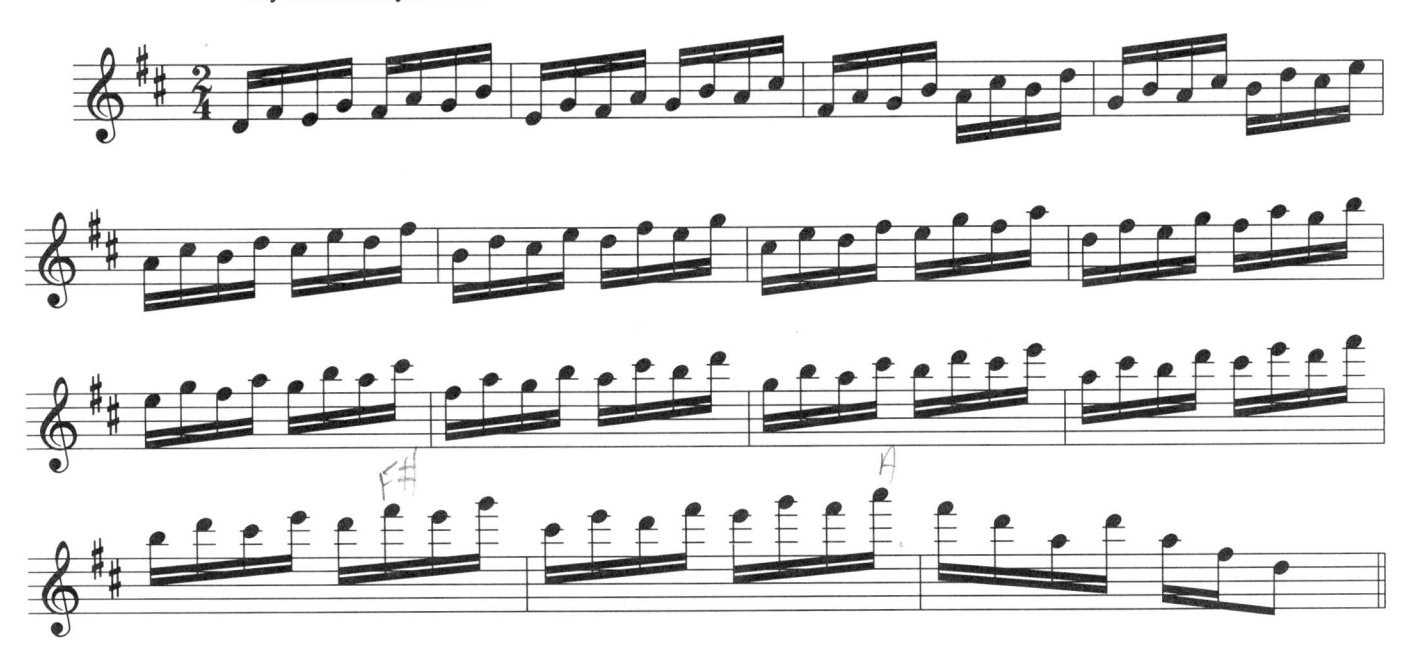

Exercise 16

Try to play each exercise with one breath

Etc.

Etc.

Etc.

106

Ex. 16 pg. 2

Ex. 16 pg. 3

Ex. 16   pg. 4

Ex. 16   pg. 5

Exercise 17

Try to play each exercise with one breath

Ex. 17 pg. 2

Ex. 17   pg. 3

Ex. 17 pg. 4

Ex. 17   pg. 5

Any articulation you desire

Any articulation you desire

Exercise 18

Try to play each exercise with one breath

Ex. 18 pg. 2

Ex. 18 pg. 3

Ex. 18 pg. 4

Ex. 18 pg. 5

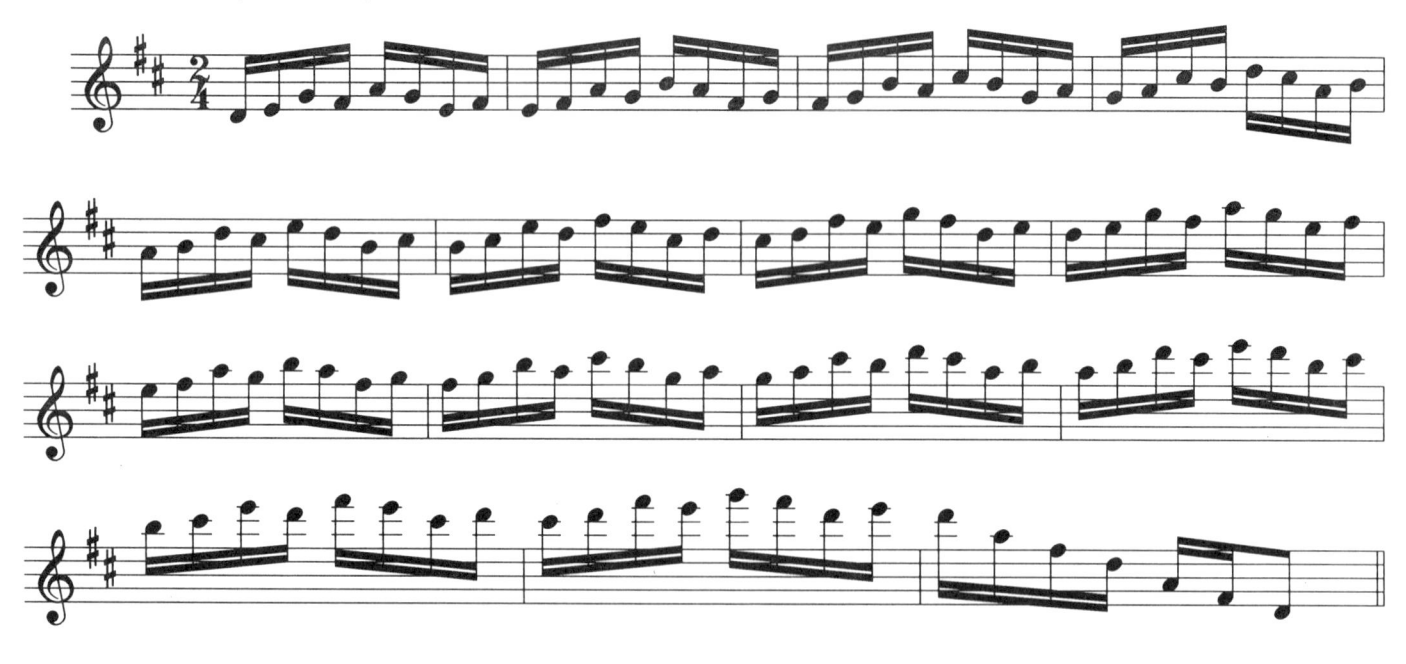

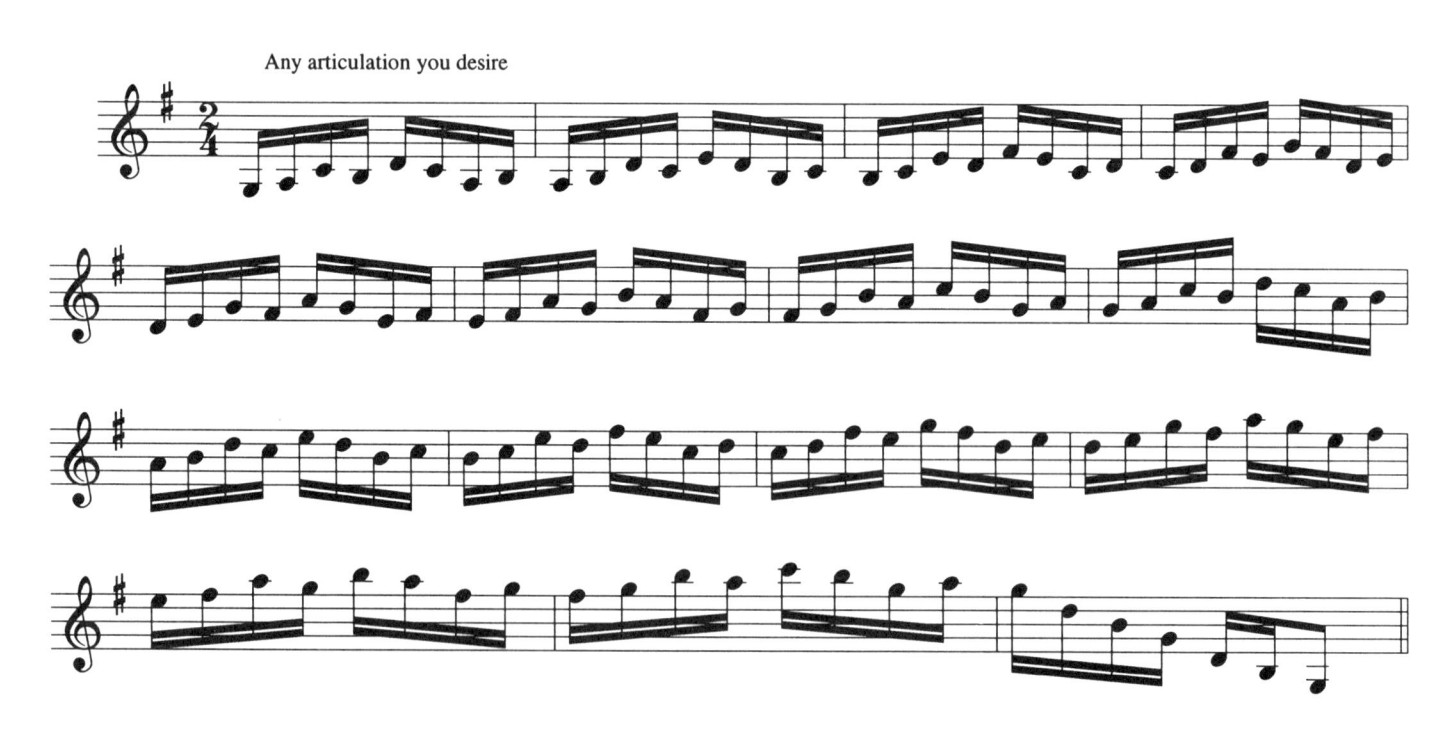

Exercise 19

Ex. 19 pg. 2

Ex. 19   pg. 3

Ex. 19 pg. 4

Ex. 19 pg. 5

Ex. 19 pg. 6

Ex. 19 pg. 7

Ex. 19 pg. 8

Ex. 19 pg. 9

Ex. 19　pg. 10

Ex. 19 pg. 11

Ex. 19 pg. 12

Any articulation you desire

Exercise 20

Ex. 20 pg. 2

Ex. 20 pg. 3

Ex. 20 pg. 4

Ex. 20 pg. 5

Ex. 20 pg. 6

Ex. 20　pg. 7

Ex. 20   pg. 8

Ex. 20 pg. 9

Ex. 20 pg. 10

Ex. 20 pg. 11

Ex. 20   pg. 12

Any articulation you desire

Chromatic Exercises

Chromatic Ex. pg. 2

Chromatic Ex. pg. 3

Chromatic Ex. pg. 4

Chromatic Ex. pg. 5

Chromatic Ex. pg. 6

Chromatic Ex. pg. 7

Section E

Modern Jazz Improvising

We are now going to utilize the melody and altered chords to act as a framework for us to devise or invent a "line" by ear, ad-lib (extemporaneously), and try to put into it a jazz pulse or jazz interpretation. To attain the modern jazz sound, we want to improvise a line that is not "choppy" but rather one that is flowing in character. At the same time, we want our invention to have a swing or pulse.

To give variety, color and interest to our line, we will not confine ourselves merely to the notes of the "spelled out" chords, but will employ also passing tones, neighboring tones, etc., keeping them within the framework of the tonality of the given chords. The line must be flowing, rhythmical.

To be effective, the line must also be played with expression, which will require, at times, the judicious use of vibrato. Whether you do or do not use vibrato in playing a given passage will depend on the interpretation desired.

On reed instruments such as the clarinet and saxophone, the vibrato is produced by a movement of the lower lip. To develop control of vibrato, I suggest daily practicing of the following. Begin with a straight tone, start the vibrato moving slowly, steadily increase its speed until you are playing a fast vibrato, then decrease slowly back to the straight line. This procedure will enable you to develop control so that at will, you can play with a straight tone, with a slow vibrato, or with a fast vibrato.

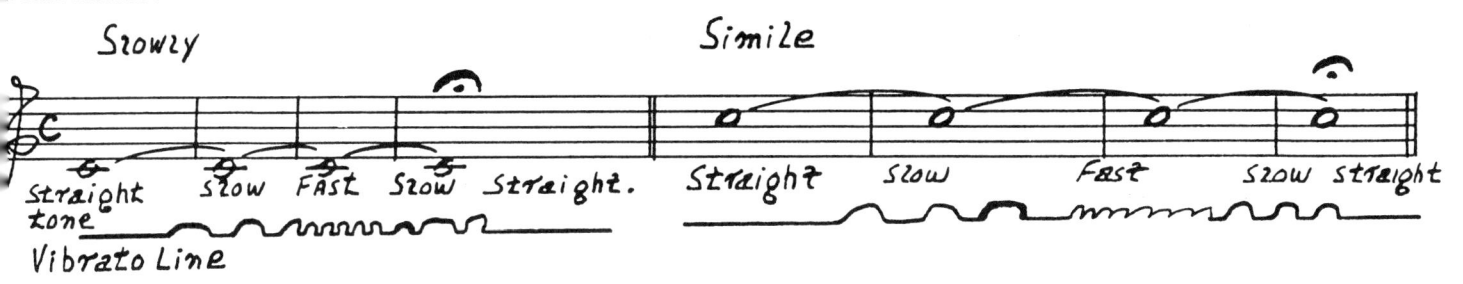

In the field of jazz, we have compositions or songs of various types and lengths. To prepare for the practical application of the improvising process, we need to examine the "form" and the harmonic structure of the composition on which we will base our improvised line.

The simplest jazz form for us to use first is a twelve-measure construction called "the blues." We will show the construction of the blues in terms of its chord progression in the key of F. To refresh your memory regarding this key, take the following test.

In the spaces provided, add in the notes to complete the chords indicated by the chord symbols, in the same manner as shown for the F major chord.

Write in an F major scale

Write in a melodic D minor scale

Write in a harmonic D minor scale

Write in an F whole-tone scale

Here are the answers to the test.

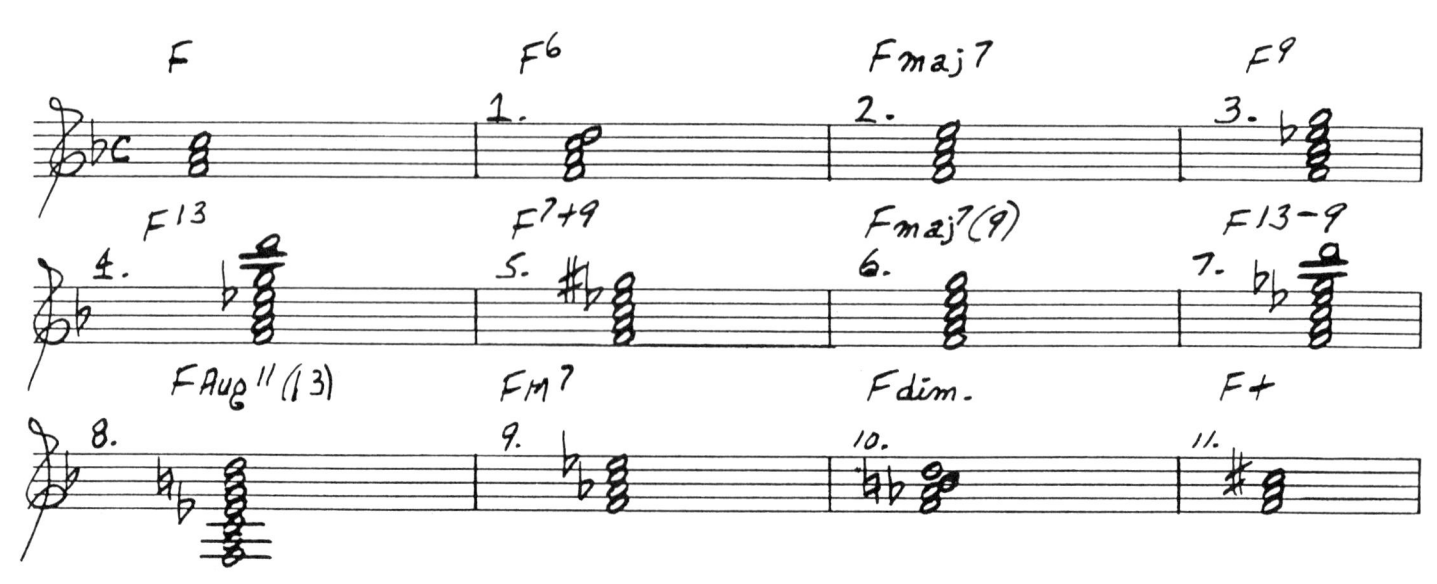

F major scale

Melodic D minor scale

Harmonic D minor scale

F whole-tone scale

Here we have the twelve-measure blues form shown in the key of F, with a fairly simple harmonization. Each diagonal stroke in the staff shows one beat.

Now we will show how a more complex and interesting harmonization can be developed on this blues foundation by the use of alternate chords and more frequent chord changes.

This example shows how you can utilize altered or alternate chords on any given chord structure. Carefully compare this harmonization with the simple one first shown.

Now we will work with a blues progression in the key of C. It is important for you to realize that if the clarinet plays in C, the piano plays in the key of Bb. The key in which the piano plays is always called the "concert key."

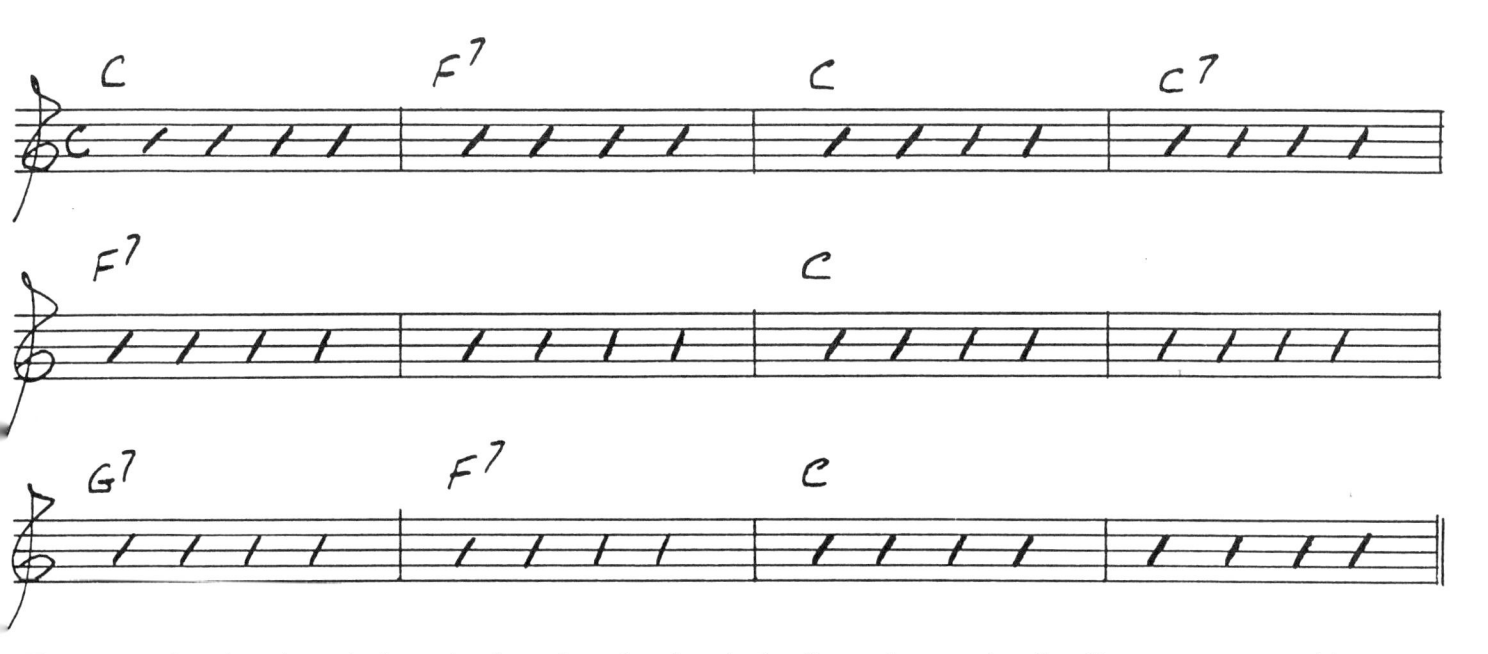

Here we employ altered or substitute chords, and we also show both a first and a second ending. Be sure to compare this with the simple progression just given, so you can get an idea of how the complex progression is developed from and related to the simple.

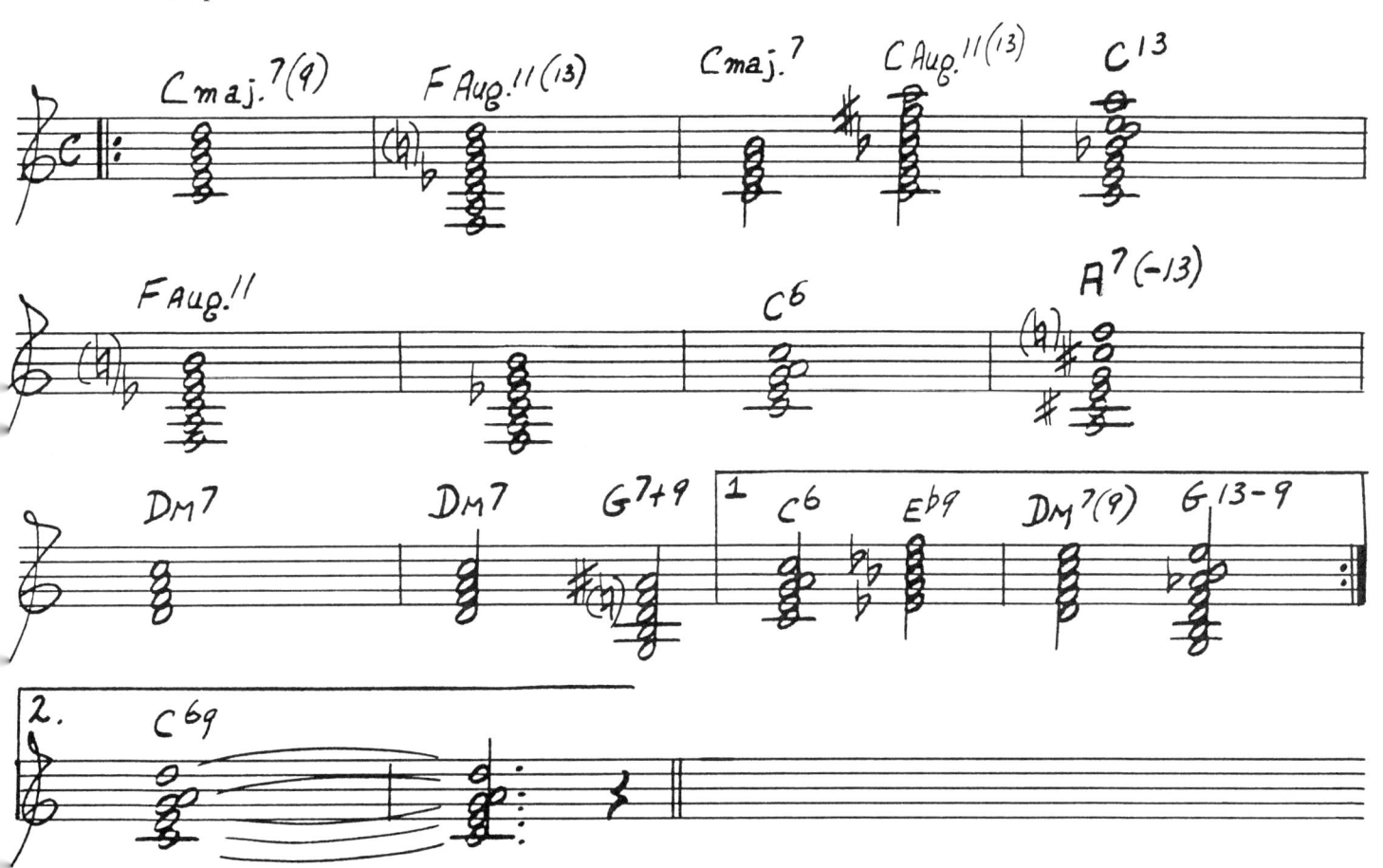

Now we will have a slightly different version of the blues progression to which we will add a melodic line. This is a simple, syncopated melody, but one combining the many elements of rhythm, accent, style, use of passing tones, etc. that together constitute modern jazz. After stating the melody, we will provide for an ad-lib solo (you may use this portion two or more times), after which you return to the given melodic line.

If you have carefully studied and absorbed the ideas given so far in this book, no doubt you will come up with one or more quite acceptable solos. However, if your first attempts turn out to be less than a highly polished, finished product, rest assured that with perseverence you will develop the ability to play ad-lib solos with confidence and authority. This is a skill that can be developed to its fullest only through many hours of thoughtful application.

It is an unalterable fact that every jazz musician should know the basic blues progression (chord changes). However, it would not be appropriate for us to go into the subject of the interpretation of the blues as such, since that is in the realm of "concept" and the history of jazz music. We will deal only with the *mechanics* of the blues.

Along with this next blues progression, I have also provided a piano part with the chord symbols (in concert key, of course) and a bass part. You might, if you have an opportunity, try these with your friends.

Blues progression with melodic line.

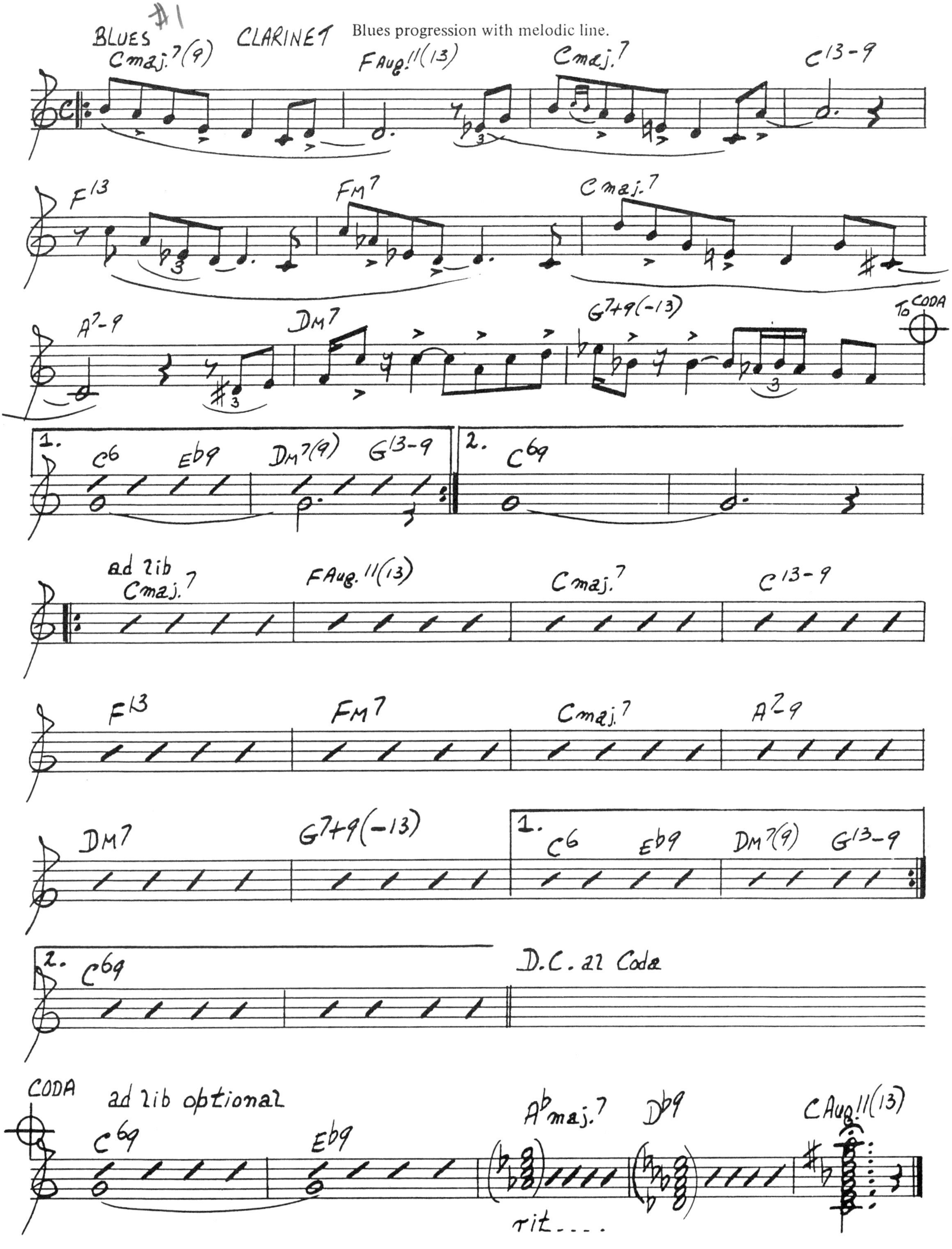

PIANO BLUES

BASS BLUES

Here is another melodic line based on a blues progression, this time in D (C concert). It might be useful to utilize the "double-time feeling" on this one if you play it at a slow tempo, for example:

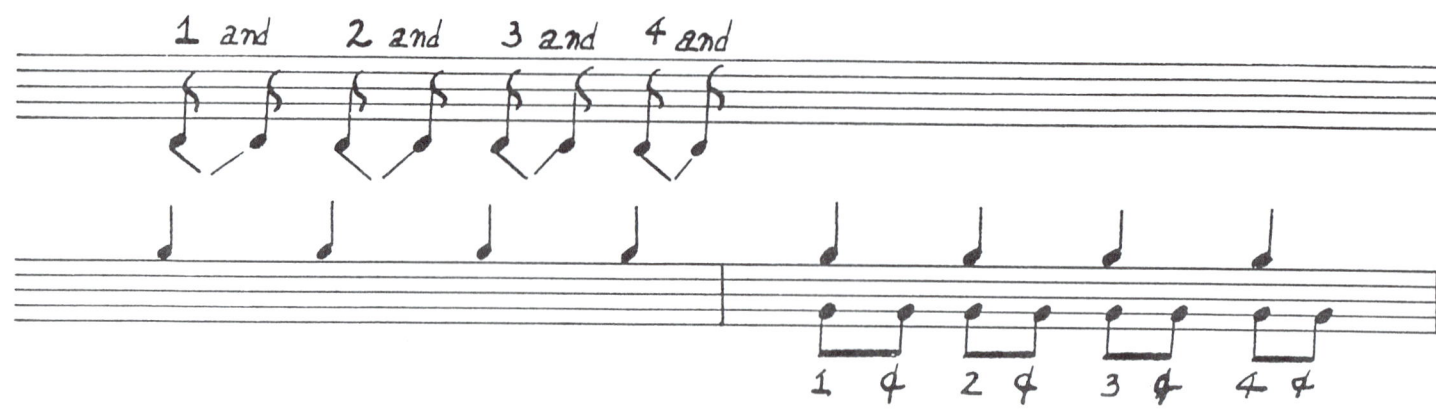

As you did before, play the line first and then play as many choruses as desired "ad-lib" and then return to the basic theme.

1.
D B7-9 Em7 A13-9
C A7-9 Dm7 G13-9
2.
D13
C13
ad lib D13 G9 D13
C13 F9 C13
G9 D13 B7+9
F9 C13 A7+9
Em7 G9 D B7-9 Em7 A13-9
Dm7 F9 C A7-9 Dm7 G13-9
D.S. AL CODA
CODA
Em7 G9 D G9 D13
Dm7 F9 C F9 C13

Here are a few recommendations for your guidance.

1. Give notes full value unless otherwise indicated.

2. Concentrate on producing a robust, vibrant tone.

3. Bear in mind always to invent the "line." In other words, think horizontally ⟶ as well as vertically ↗ ↘ ↗

4. Use the straight tone or tone with vibrato to the maximum benefit.

5. Use discretion in the choice of altered chords so that full use can be made of harmonic tension.

6. Try to coordinate your mental or intellectual faculties with your physical pulse or swing. That is to say, don't freeze up because you're thinking, and don't resort to gimmicks or bad tone or become a "one note" artist because "you're swingin'." (Swinging one note has it's effective use at the right place.)

Now a few words about the "short quarter-note" and the "long eighth-note" in jazz. Where two or more quarter-notes occur in succession at a slow or medium tempo, they should usually be played with less than full value. This is particularly true when the notes are shown with accents.

These quarter-notes, at a medium or slow tempo

would ordinarily be played in this manner in a stage band or with a jazz group.

This interpretation is less than a general rule so we must be prepared to determine what the composer or arranger wants, using our "musical senses."

This inter pretation is less than a general rule so we must be prepared to determine what the composer or arranger wants, using our "musical sense."

We have given a good deal of consideration to the blues form. Now we will examine some of the larger forms suitable for jazz. Among the standards frequently used as a basis for playing jazz you will find a comparatively few consisting of 16 measures and other lengths less than 32 measures. However, by far the majority of these compositions or songs are 32 measures in length. Actually, these popular and jazz songs can be almost any number of measures in length. We want to familiarize you with the construction or form of some of the more conventional.

The 32 measure form or construction consists of:

a – an 8 measure theme ending in such a way that the ear knows there is more to come, leading into

b – An 8 measure theme frequently identical to the opening theme, except that it has a closing with more of a feeling of finality.

c – an 8 measure theme usually somewhat contrasting in character and frequently more complex in its harmonies, called the "bridge" which leads to

d – An 8 measure theme usually consisting of a restatement of the original theme and having a close with a feeling of finality. This last section can come to a deceptive closing at the end of 8 measures and reach a final closing only after the addition of 2 or sometimes 4 or more measures.

Or, the 32 measure construction can be:

a – an 8 measure theme, incomplete of itself, and leading to

b – a second 8 measure passage which is actually a continuation, followed by

c – an 8 measure restatement of the opening theme leading into

d – another 8 measure passage which completes the song, this passage usually only partly resembling the second 8 measure section.

Where a section of a song closes in such a way that you know more of it is to follow, we will call this closing a "first ending." Almost invariably, the final chord of a first ending is basically a dominant seventh chord on V, the dominant of the key. This chord, in modern jazz, appears as an alteration and/or extension of the dominant seventh chord. At the end of the entire song, if the song is to be repeated, we have a similarly constructed first ending.

A section within a song can end with a considerable feeling of finality, this type of ending being called a "second ending." The end of the entire song, except if it is to be repeated, will be in the nature of a second ending. The final chord of a second ending is usually an alteration and/or extension of a major chord on I, the tonic of the key.

Here are a few examples of the first ending or "turn around" used in modern jazz, shown in the key of C.

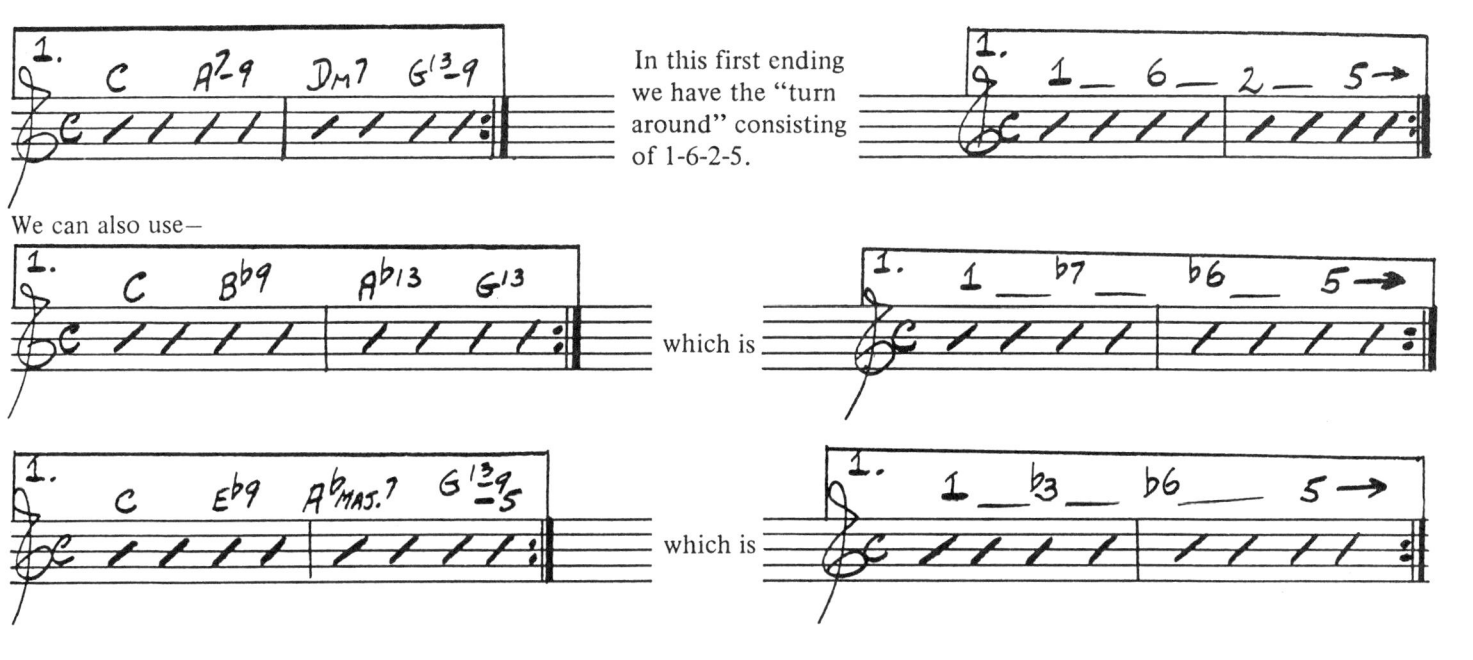

In this first ending we have the "turn around" consisting of 1-6-2-5.

We can also use—

which is

which is

These are just a few of the possibilities.

Here are a few typical second endings.

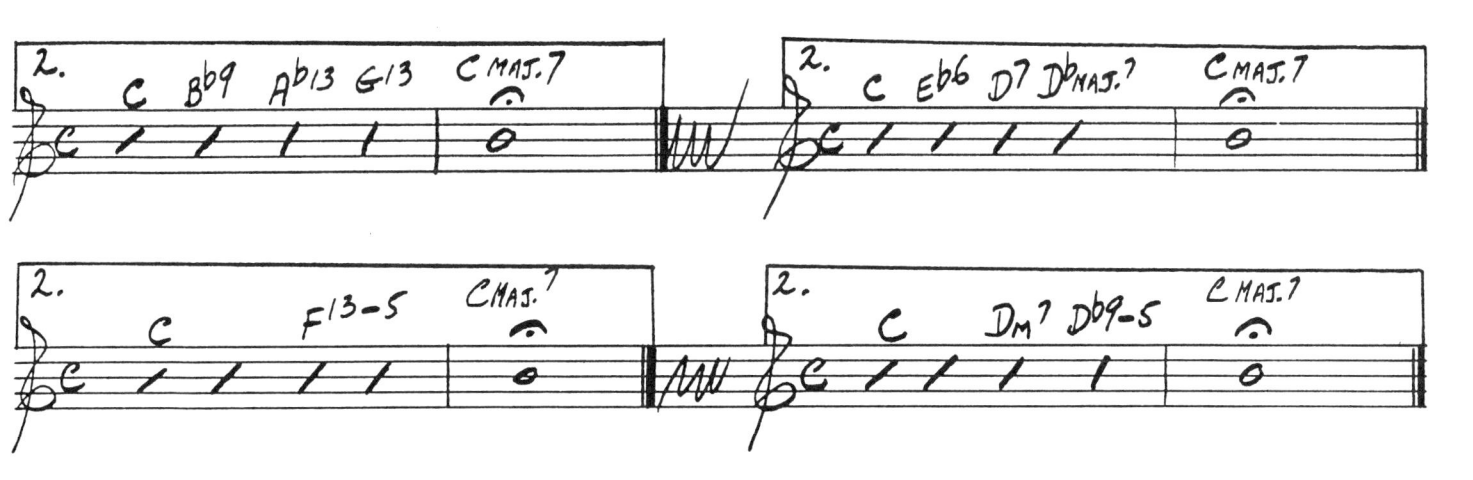

Now to songs consisting of more than 32 measures. The 44 measure construction usually consists of:

a — a 12 measure theme having a first ending, leading to

b — a 12 measure theme having a second ending, and then

c — an 8 measure bridge similar in structure and character to the bridge of a 32 measure form, and finally

d — a 12 measure section consisting usually of a restatement of the opening theme.

The 64 measure form is usually:

a — a 16 measure theme having a first ending, leading to

b — a 16 measure theme having a second ending, and then

c — a 16 measure bridge, and finally

d — a 16 measure section consisting usually of a restatement of the opening theme.

There are, of course, a great many songs unusual in their type of construction and having unusual numbers of measures.

At this point we will have another test, this time in the key of G. Add the notes to complete the chords indicated by the chord symbols.

1. G
2. G⁷
3. G⁹
4. G¹³
5. Gm⁷
6. Gm⁷⁻⁵
7. G¹³⁻⁹
8. Gmaj.⁷⁽⁹⁾
9. G⁷⁺⁹
10. G+
11. G dim.
12. G⁷⁻⁹⁽⁻¹³⁾
13. G Aug.¹¹
14. G Aug¹¹⁽¹³⁾

Add the note to construct the indicated interval.

15. Major 3rd
16. Perfect 5th
17. Minor 3rd
18. Major 6th
19. Minor 6th
20. Minor 7th
21. Major 7th
22. Major 10th
23. Aug. 9th
24. Major 9th
25. Aug. 4th
26. Dim. 5th
27. Minor 2nd
28. Major 2nd
29. Perfect 4th
30. Minor 9th
31. Perfect 11th
32. Aug 11th

See answers on next page.

Here are the answers to the test.

Next we have a melody in the key of G. This is to be used, as before, by playing the melody as written, then playing an ad-lib chorus, and finally again playing the melody as it appears. This is a 32 measure construction consisting of an 8 measure theme repeated, an 8 measure bridge, and finally a restatement of the opening 8 measure theme.

1. Bm7　E7-9	Am7　D13 :		2. Bm7	D13　G6
Dm7	G13	C6	/
Dm7	G13	C6	/
Em7	A13	Am7	D13
G6　G#dim.	Am7　A#dim.	Bm7　E7-9	Am7　D13
Dm7　G13-9	C　Cm7	Bm7	D13　G6 || *D.C. al Coda*

CODA

| Bm7 | D13　G6 ||

Here is a test in the key of D.

1. Write the first inversion of a D major triad.

2. Write the dominant seventh chord in the key of D major.

3. Play an F# major scale from memory.

4. What is the submediant in the key of D major?

5. What is the relative minor to D major?

6. Write the dominant seventh chord in the key of D major, and its resolution.

Add in the notes to complete the chords indicated by the chord symbols.

7. D dim.   8. D aug.¹¹   9. D aug.¹¹⁽¹³⁾   10. D+

Play the following exercise at a bright tempo.

Here are the answers to the test.

1.
2.
3.

4. The submediant is B.

5. The relative minor is B minor.

Dominant seventh chord
A7

Resolution
D

6.

7. D dim.   8. D aug.11   9. D aug.11(13)   10. D+

The next melodic line uses the minor mode against the basic blues progression. Here we can employ the Dorian modal scales.

Notice that in the first measure, if you add some of the notes used in the melodic line to the notes of the D major chord, you have the chord D7+9. In carrying out this procedure, we need to consider that F and E# sound the same pitch (called "enharmonic equivalents"). In effect, you have added an F major chord (in its second inversion) above a D major chord. Notice that we are doubling the A already present in the D major chord. The F chord is said to be "superimposed" upon the D chord.

D   add   F   becomes   D7+9

Here we have a situation which we may call "polychordal" (two or more chords being employed simultaneously). For our purpose we could also designate this as being "polytonal" (two or more tonalities being employed simultaneously). Thus, D7+9 can be considered to be F major superimposed upon D major, or F/D. It could also be considered F/D7 in which case the C♮ is common to both chords. Bear in mind, however, that the generating tone in the bass register determines the predominant chordal influence and tonality in any given measure.

In employing harmonic-melodic devices such as discussed, it is highly desirable to discuss the details with the pianist (or guitarist) playing the chord background to your improvisation. After a considerable amount of experience, you will intuitively feel when these devices may be effectively employed.

In the ad-lib portion of this music, the minor mode, the D7+9 framework and the polychordal structures may all be used.

Note: the ♭3rd and ♭7 played against a major chord referred to as "blue notes" in the early days of Jazz.

Blues

Here is another blues construction you will find interesting and useful for practical purposes.

PIANO

Medium tempo
(in unison with clarinet)

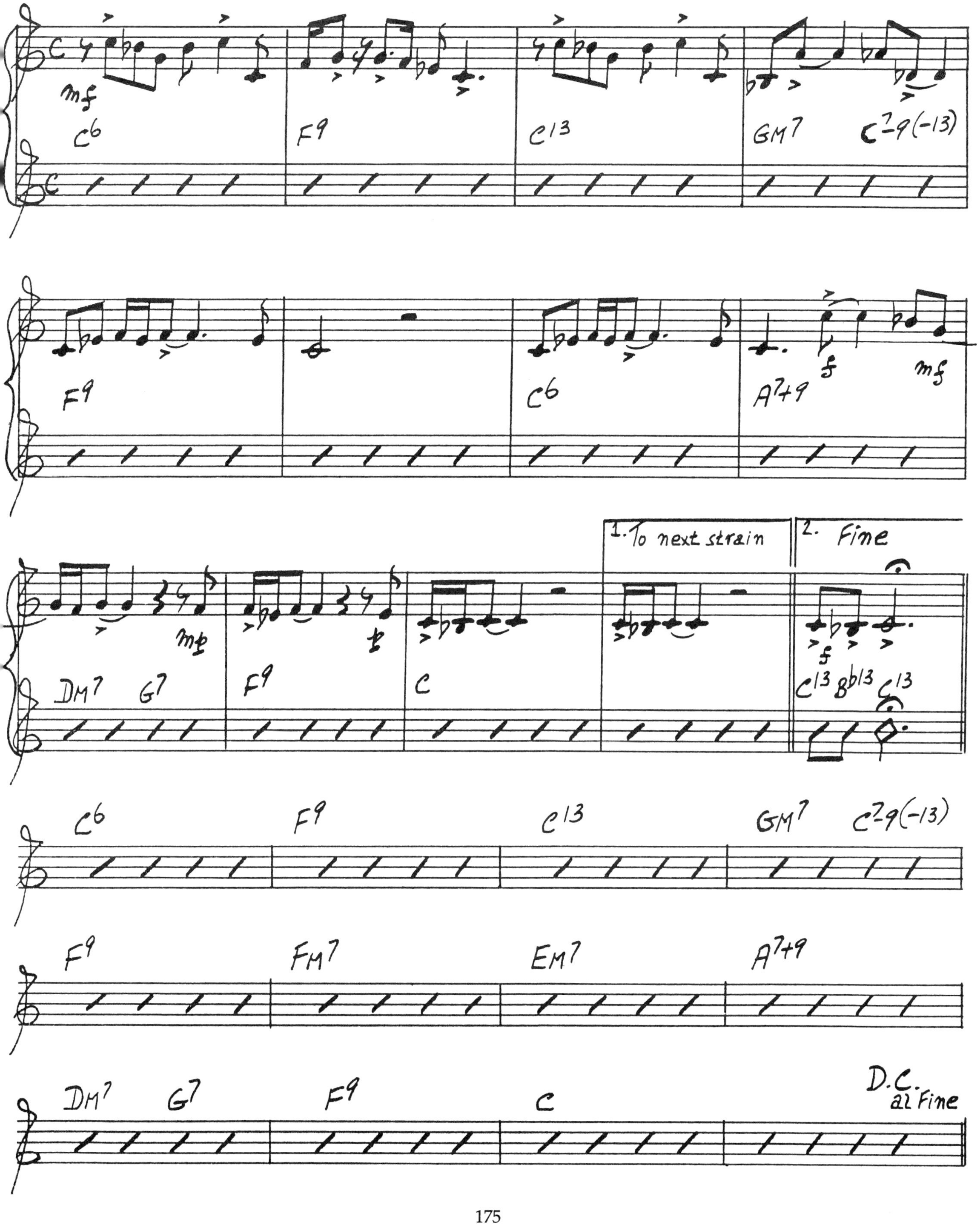

The Clarinet as Related to Concert Key

Those of you who play clarinet or other Bb instruments (trumpet, tenor saxophone) need to become familiar with the relationship of their instruments to concert key, the key in which piano, accordian, guitar and many other instruments play. When you sound C on your instrument, you are playing Bb concert. This will enable you to call a key signature or chord progression to a pianist or accordionist or guitarist, or recognize them when they are called to you in concert key. For instance, if the first three chords of any given tune are C, Cm7, F7 for your instrument, you need to know that the pianist will play Bb, Bbm7, Eb7.

Many times chord symbols are written out on your part in concert key, so you must be able to transpose these chords to your key. The following music, shown only as a chord progression, is in F concert (G for you). See if you can read the chord symbols, transposing each of them one step (a major 2nd) higher and invent your own solo (in the key of G) based on this progression. To help you get started, we have shown under the music the first few chord symbols transposed into your key. If you can't read these chords at a moderate tempo, go back and study your chord symbols more thoroughly.

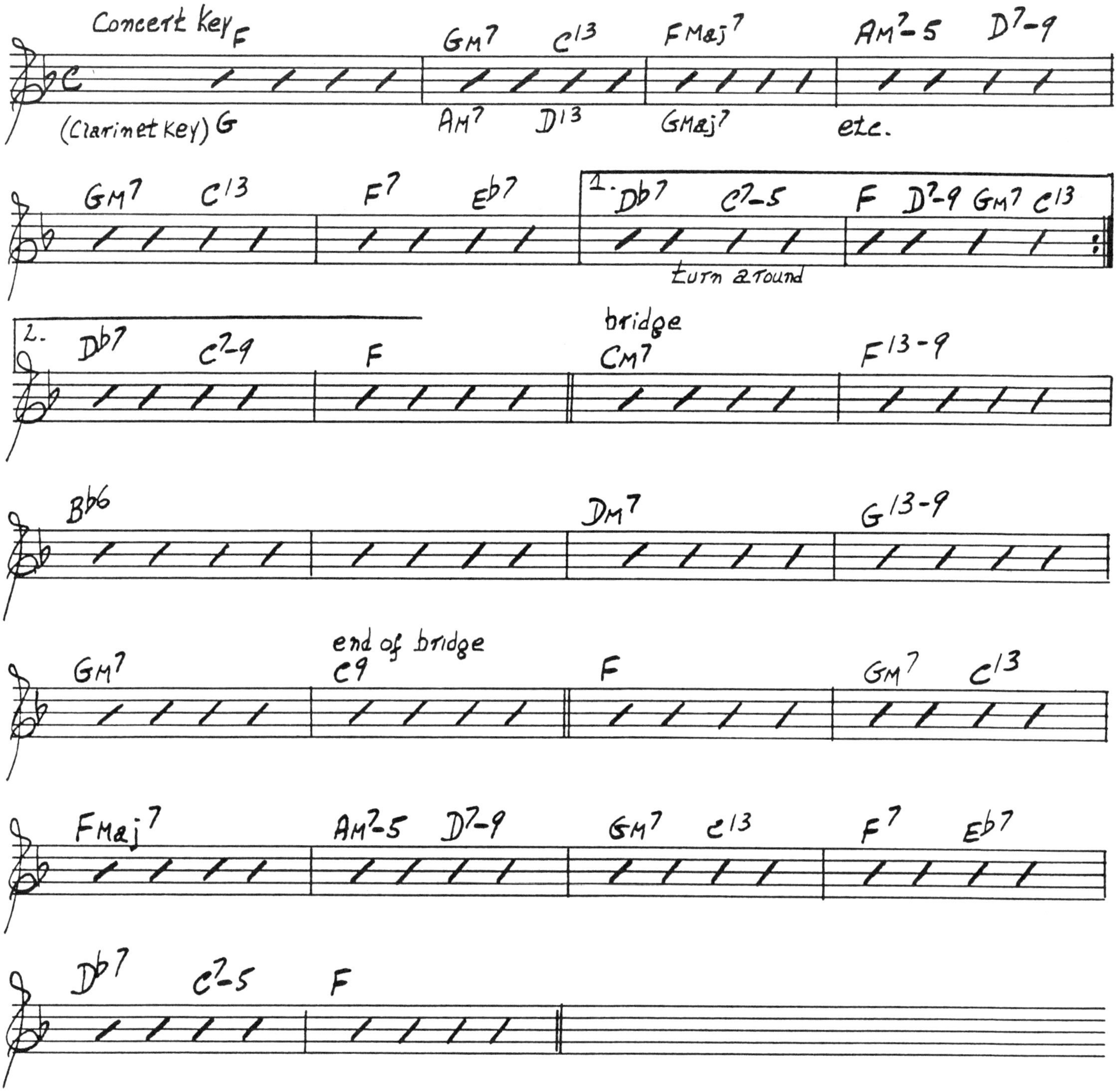
Concert key F
(Clarinet key) G
GM7 C13
AM7 D13
FMaj7
GMaj7
AM7-5 D7-9
etc.
GM7 C13
F7 Eb7
1. Db7 C7-5
F D7-9 GM7 C13
turn around
2. Db7 C7-9
F
bridge
CM7
F13-9
Bb6
DM7
G13-9
GM7
end of bridge
C9
F
GM7 C13
FMaj7
AM7-5 D7-9
GM7 C13
F7 Eb7
Db7 C7-5
F

Again we will turn our attention to polytonal and polychordal writing. It is only comparatively recently that modern jazz composers have utilized these devices to enable the ad-lib soloist to take a choice of two or more tonalities in which to improvise on the same composition. When playing in this field of music, it goes without saying that the soloist must choose his notes carefully in order to achieve desirable results.

In order to communicate their ideas with clarity, many composers who want a polychordal effect are writing dual chord symbols showing the basic chord below and the superimposed chord above. For instance, instead of writing C7+9, they will show Eb/C7. Below we show some examples of the many possibilities of polychordal structures, the dual chord symbols being indicated.

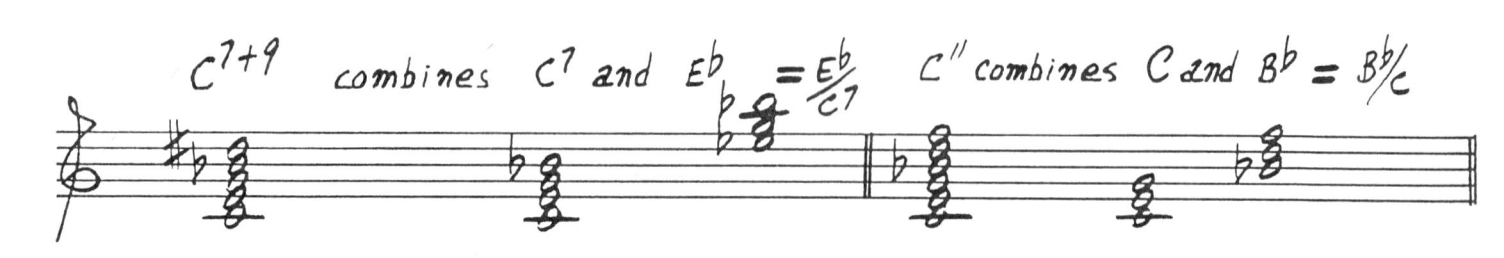

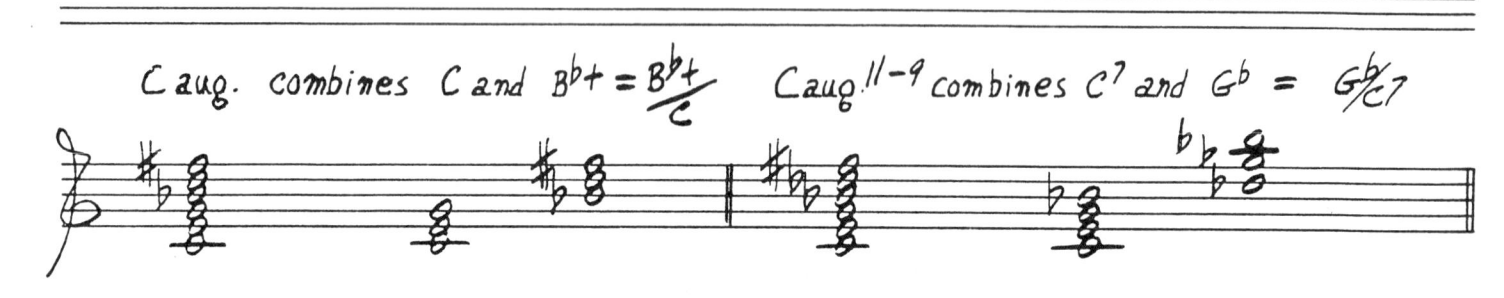

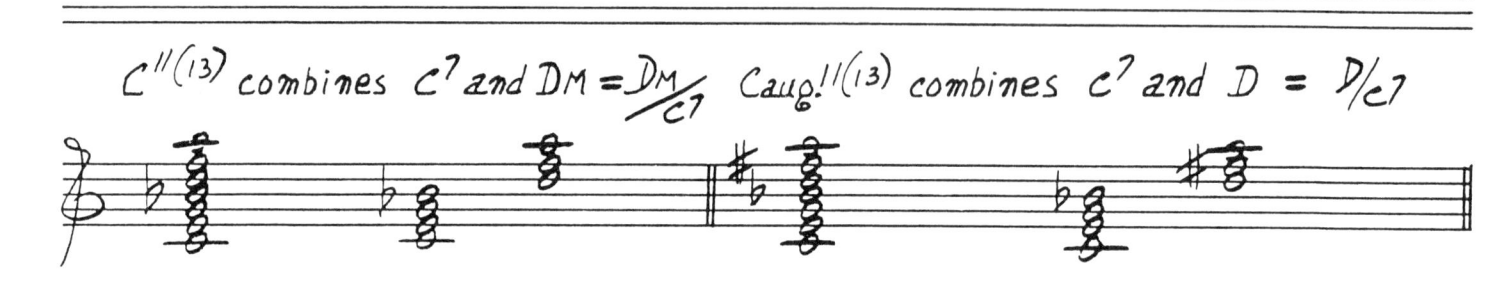

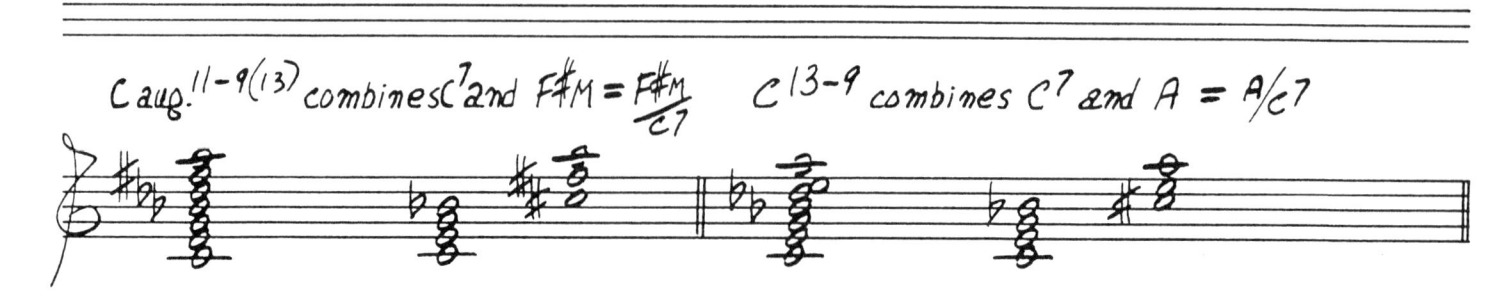

Here we show the practical application. The piano plays a Bb7 chord, which is C7 for clarinet. Several examples are given in the clarinet part showing various chords superimposed. The component chords are shown, also the symbol of the chord which combines the basic and the superimposed chords.

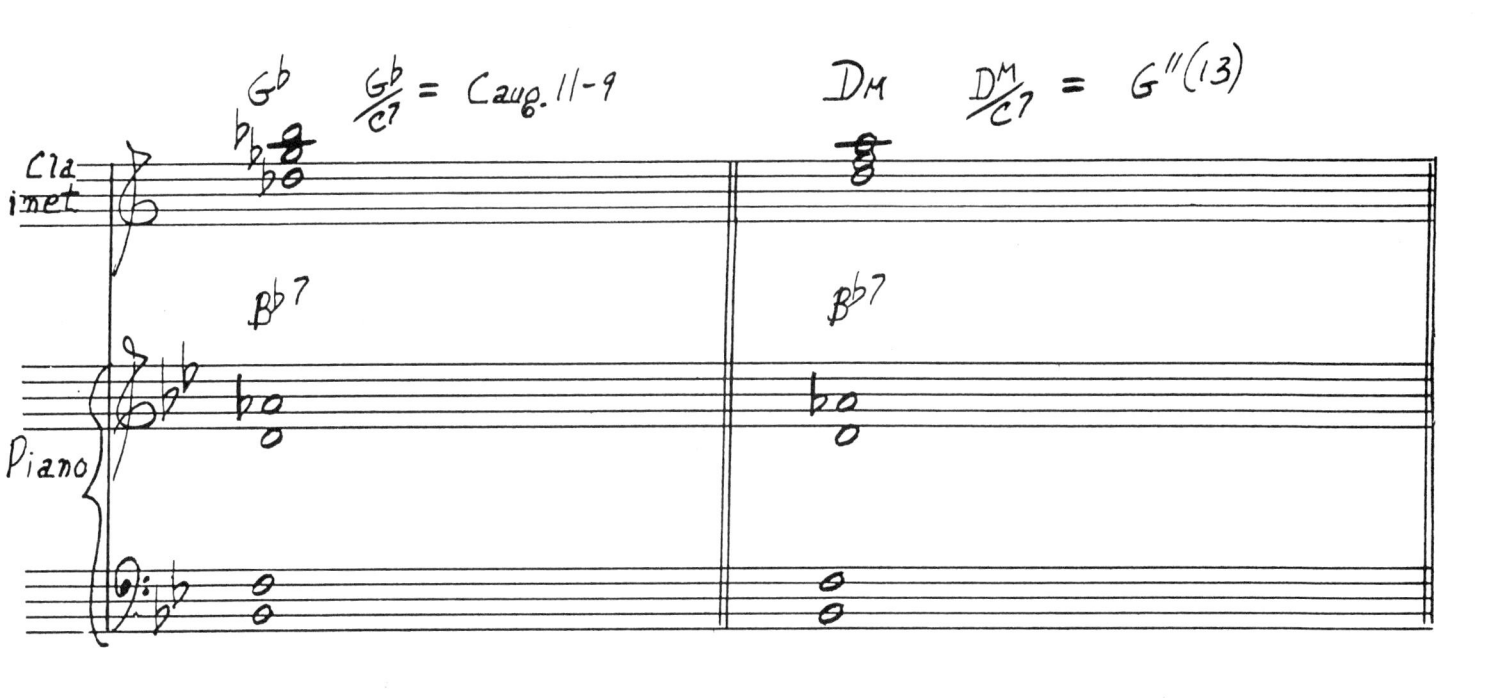

Now we will give some consideration to modern jazz as played in meters other than four-four time. The past years have brought about new concepts of jazz solo and orchestration not only in the basic four-four time but also in three-four and five-four. We will consider first the three-four "swing."

The rhythm section plays an important role here. Its members must provide a "swing" or "four-beat-like pulse" but keep the meter in three-four.

The bassist may not necessarily accent the first beat of each measure as he would in playing a waltz—

Rather, he should play each note in the three-four idiom evenly and swing each note as though he were actually playing in four-four, like this—

The drummer may use a variety of rhythmic patterns. The following are some examples.

On his big cymbal he may play—

and on his sock cymbal he may play—

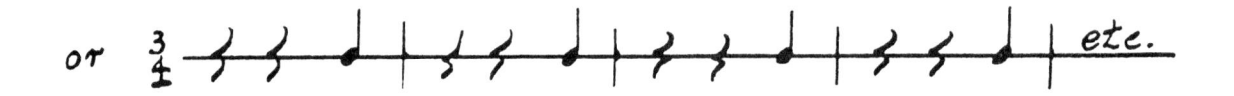

The pianist may play his chord background or "comping" as it is customarily called, in this manner—

The very same ideas apply to the playing of five-four jazz.

We may feel five-four by dividing the measure in this way—

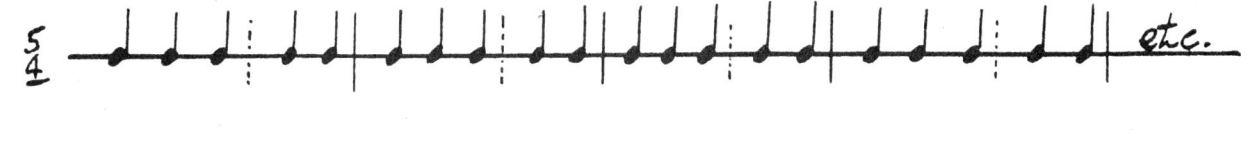

or this—

Now we will show something of polyrhythmic ideas. Here is an example—show various rhythms that can be used simultaneously where the meter is basically four beats to the measure—

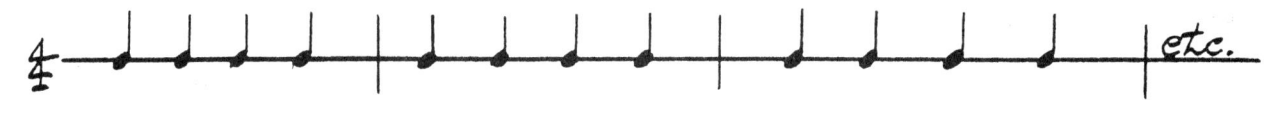

Concluding Remarks

During recent years I have found the tendency among musicians and critics alike to fall into certain categories, such as "cool" school, "soul" jazz, "hard" swing, "third stream," "be-bop," West Coast jazz, Dixie, swing, modern Dixie, "modified bop," "free form," etc. It is my belief that we must be more flexible in our taste regarding what we listen to. Simply because we prefer to play and listen to "cool jazz" does not mean we can't learn from all accomplished jazz artists. What we prefer to play is one thing, but we must recognize that there is value in other schools of thought.

This fact became obvious to me during one of the many times I had the great honor to work with Charlie Parker. We were doing a show with a local band consisting mostly of Dixieland players. Naturally, I anticipated some friction. To my surprise, Charlie played all the Dixieland "charts" and knew them and played them well. No doubt he didn't make a practice of this, but it was certainly an enjoyable musical event for all of us.

It is my firm belief that in the final analysis what we produce musically is the sum total of all that we have heard and all that we have absorbed emotionally. All of this crystallizes into the ability to project a jazz feeling. Of course in addition to this is our own initiative and drive, and our own inventive qualities.

Many students ask me if it is wise to copy well-known artists in the field. I would say in the beginning, yes up to a point. We all need influences. No one, regardless of his talents and creative ability, can say that he was not influenced by anyone else.

It is, however, a mistake to copy "verbatim" what someone else has done without the initiative and curiosity that is necessary to begin developing our own lines in our own individual way. In the case of many of our younger jazz exponents, it is most unfortunate that they copy so well that they are not readily identifiable. That is, they sound like imitations of some well-known artist who, by the way, spent many hours and days and years to develop, only to have his contribution diluted or nullified by so many "brain pickers."

It is up to us, therefore, to investigate our innermost feelings and perceptions to determine in which way we will most successfully bring to the surface our own specific way of saying something musically.

The following piece is based on familiar chord combinations. Our objective here is to play through these lines (by the way, the "melody" of these compositions are usually referred to as "head" or "line") and chords with fluency and ease.

Tone – Quality
Articulation
Inflection

Harmonic sense

Melodic sense

Rhythmic feel

Max Is Back

Max Is Back

Pg 2.

CLAR. ad lib Solo

| Gm7 | Cm7 | F13 | Bb |

| Cm7 | Em7 A13-9 | D | D |

| Dm | Gm | C13 | F |

| Gm7 | E7+9 | A | A |

Bridge

| Bm7-5 | E7 | A | A |

| Abm7-5 | C#7-9 | F# | D+ |

| Gm7 | Cm7 | F13 | Bb |

| Eb | EbM7 Ab7 | Dm7 | DbM7 Gb7 |

| Cm7 | Cm7 | Bb | Am7-5 D7-9 | back to "head"

Max Is Back

Max Is Back

Pg. 2.

PIANO
Clar. 2d rib solo

FM7	B♭M7	E♭13	A♭
B♭M7	Dm7 G13-9	C	C
CM	FM	B♭13	E♭
FM7	D7+9	G	G

BRIDGE
| Am7-5 | D7 | G | G |
| G♭M7-5 | B7-9 | E | C+ |

FM7	B♭M7	E♭13	A♭
F	D♭M7 G♭7	Cm7	Bm7 E7
B♭M7	B♭M7 E♭13-9 A♭	Gm7-5 C7-9	back to "head"

BASS

Max Is Back

Max Is Back

Bass — pg. 2

Fm7	B♭m7	E♭13	A♭
Bbm7	Dm7 G13-9	C	C
Cm	Fm	B♭13	E♭
Fm7	D7+9	G	G

BRIDGE

Am7-5	D7	G	G
G♭m7-5	B7-9	E	C+
Fm7	B♭m7	E♭13	A♭
F	D♭m7 G♭7	Cm7	Bm7 E7
B♭m7	B♭m7 E♭13-9 A♭	Gm7-5 C7-9 back to "head"

DRUMS
Max Is Back

Lake Five

Lake Five

Lake Five

Lake Five

Chloe's Odyssey

Chloe's Odyssey

CLAR. P. 2

TO CODA

D Solo AD LIB

G	E7+9
Am7	C#m7 F#7 Dm7	G7♭9	C
Cm7 F7 G	B♭7+11	Am7	D13♭9

1. | G | B♭7 | E♭maj.7 | D7♭9 |

2. | G | % | Fm7 | B♭7 |

E♭	C7♭9	Fm7	E♭/B♭	Gm7
F#m7	Fm7	B♭13	E♭	G7+9
CM	%	Am7 D7	B♭m7 E♭7
Am7 D13	G	E7+9 Am7	C#m7 F#7
Dm7	G7♭9	C	Cm7 F7 G

Chloe's Odyssey

Chloe's Odyssey

Chloe's Odyssey

PIANO P. 3

Chloe's Odyssey

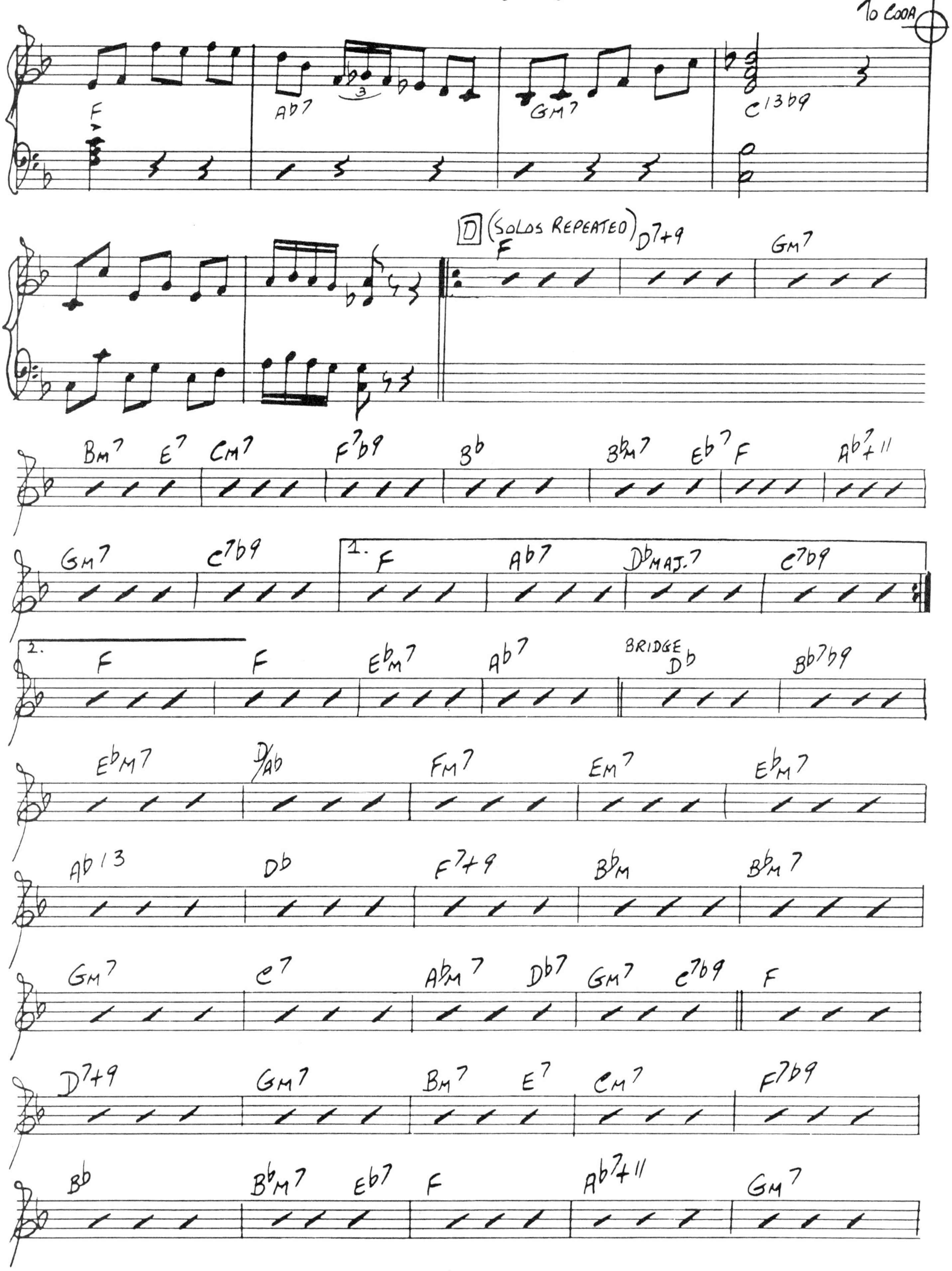

Chloe's Odyssey

Piano P. 4

Chloe's Odyssey

Chloe's Odyssey

Chloe's Odyssey

Buddy De Franco

CLAR.

Flathead Blues

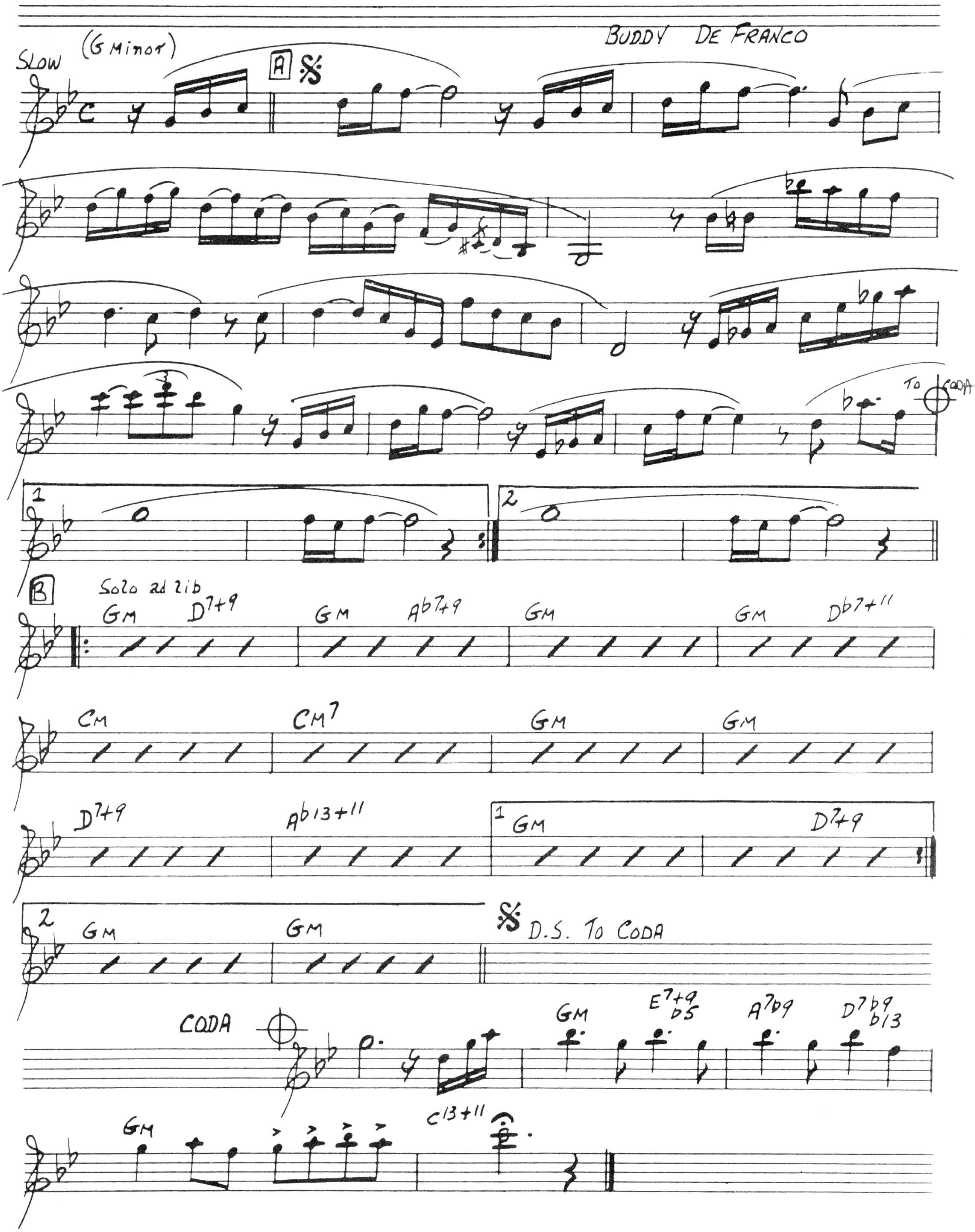

Flathead Blues

Buddy DeFranco

Flathead Blues

Flathead Blues

Flathead Blues